COOKBOOK & RECIPE CARDS

Publications
International, Ltd.

Pictured on the front cover (clockwise from top): Cucumber and Onion Salad *(page 28)*, Berry Simple Smoothie *(page 89)*, Sand Tarts *(page 50)*, and Fresh Strawberry Pie *(page 78)*.

Pictured on the back cover: Frozen Mini Cinnamon Coffee Cheesecakes *(page 76)*.

ISBN-13: 978-1-60553-355-1
ISBN-10: 1-60553-355-6

Library of Congress Control Number: 2009935949

Manufactured in China.

8 7 6 5 4 3 2 1

Nutritional Analysis: Every effort has been made to check the accuracy of the nutritional information that appears with each recipe. However, because numerous variables account for a wide range of values for certain foods, nutritive analyses in this book should be considered approximate. Different results may be obtained by using different nutrient databases and different brand-name products.

Publications
International, Ltd.

Recipes to Share

Every cook loves to impress his or her guests with delicious recipes—and there's no better compliment than being asked for a copy of the recipe. SPLENDA® *Cookbook & Recipe Cards* is the perfect resource for preparing the ultimate dish, then sharing the recipe with your family and friends.

Forty-eight delicious, classic recipes await you, each with step-by-step instructions and a mouthwatering photo of the final dish. And for each recipe, you'll also find a recipe card to tear out and share with others.

Cinnamon-Pecan Monkey Bread and Polynesian Pork Chops may entice you, or how about Old Fashioned Peanut Butter Chocolate Chip Cookies or S'mores Campfire Pie—a family favorite? You may also enjoy a Caramel Latte for yourself or serving a Berry Simple Smoothie to your children. Or, why not make Nostalgic Apple Pie a part of your holiday tradition?

You'll find recipes for every day and special days just waiting for you and your family and friends to enjoy.

Blueberry Corn Muffins
(page 14 and page 102)

Cookbook Contents

Breakfast &
Brunch Foods 6

Main Dishes & Sides 26

Cookies & Bites 44

Pies & Desserts 64

Beverages & Smoothies 80

Index 93

Recipe Card Contents

Breakfast &
Brunch Foods 97

Main Dishes & Sides . . . 107

Cookies & Bites 117

Pies & Desserts 127

Beverages & Smoothies . . . 135

Breakfast & Brunch Foods

Apple Pie Oatmeal

- **1 cup water**
- **½ cup old-fashioned oats**
- **1 dash salt (optional)**

Apple Pie Topping:

- **2 teaspoons SPLENDA® Brown Sugar Blend**
- **1 tablespoon chopped apple**
- **1 dash apple pie spice**

1. Stovetop Directions: Bring water to a boil in a small saucepan. Stir in oats and salt. Cook, stirring occasionally, over medium heat 5 minutes.

or

Microwave Directions: Combine water, oats and salt in a microwave-safe bowl. Cover tightly with heavy-duty plastic wrap; fold back a small edge to allow steam to escape. Microwave on high 2½ to 3 minutes; stir well.

2. Top oatmeal with SPLENDA® Brown Sugar Blend, chopped apple and spice.

Makes 1 serving

¾ cup oatmeal, 1 tablespoon sweetened chopped apple

PREP TIME: 10 minutes

TOTAL TIME: 10 minutes

Nutrition Information per Serving:
Calories 200 (25 calories from fat), Total Fat 3 g, Saturated Fat 0 g, Protein 7 g, Carbohydrate 37 g, Cholesterol 0 mg, Fiber 5 g, Sodium 400 mg, Sugars 10 g

Apricots and Ricotta Cheese Toast

1 **cup water**

½ **cup SPLENDA® Sugar Blend**

1 **vanilla bean, split lengthwise**

1 **lemon, zested**

6 **fresh apricots, peeled, halved and pitted**

1 **tablespoon butter, softened**

4 **slices bread, toasted**

1 **cup part-skim ricotta cheese**

Optional Garnish: vanilla beans

1. Preheat broiler.

2. Combine water, SPLENDA® Sugar Blend, vanilla bean and lemon zest in a non-aluminum saucepan. Bring to a boil over medium heat, stirring until SPLENDA® Sugar Blend dissolves; reduce heat and simmer 10 minutes or until mixture is reduced. Add apricots and simmer for 3 to 5 minutes or until apricots are just tender. Using a slotted spoon, remove apricots from syrup. Set aside.

3. Spread butter on bread slices. Broil until bread is lightly toasted.

4. Spoon ricotta cheese on each bread slice. Top with apricots and remaining syrup. Broil 2 to 3 minutes or until thoroughly heated and apricots begin to caramelize. Garnish with a vanilla bean, if desired. Serve immediately.

Makes 4 servings

1 slice toast, ¼ cup ricotta, 3 apricot halves, 1 tablespoon syrup

---

PREP TIME: 10 minutes

COOK TIME: 18 minutes

TOTAL TIME: 28 minutes

Nutrition Information per Serving:
Calories 340 (80 calories from fat), Total Fat 9 g, Saturated Fat 5 g, Protein 10 g, Carbohydrate 49 g, Cholesterol 25 mg, Fiber 2 g, Sodium 240 mg, Sugars 34 g

Banana Mini-Chip Muffins

2 cups all-purpose flour

2 teaspoons baking powder

½ teaspoon salt

¾ cup light butter, softened

⅓ cup SPLENDA® Sugar Blend

⅓ cup packed SPLENDA® Brown Sugar Blend

1 teaspoon vanilla extract

3 medium ripe bananas, mashed

1 large egg

1 (12-ounce) package NESTLÉ® TOLL HOUSE® Semi-Sweet Chocolate Mini Morsels

1. Preheat oven to 350°F. Spray 48 mini-muffin cups with nonstick cooking spray; set aside.

2. Combine flour, baking powder and salt in medium bowl; set aside.

3. Combine butter, SPLENDA® Sugar Blend, SPLENDA® Brown Sugar Blend and vanilla in large bowl; beat at medium speed with a mixer until creamy. Beat in bananas and egg. Gradually mix in flour mixture; stir in morsels. Spoon batter evenly into prepared pan, filling cups two-thirds full.

4. Bake 15 to 20 minutes or until a toothpick inserted in the centers comes out clean. Cool 10 minutes in pans on wire rack. Remove muffins from pans to wire rack to cool completely.

Makes 48 servings
1 mini-muffin

PREP TIME: 10 minutes

COOK TIME: 20 minutes

TOTAL TIME: 40 minutes

Nutrition Information per Serving:
Calories 90 (35 calories from fat), Total Fat 4 g, Saturated Fat 2 g, Protein 1 g, Carbohydrate 13 g, Cholesterol 10 mg, Fiber 0 g, Sodium 55 mg, Sugars 8 g

Pistachio Cranberry Scones

3 cups all-purpose flour

1½ teaspoons cream of tartar

¾ teaspoon baking soda

½ teaspoon salt

1 tablespoon orange zest

6 tablespoons butter

⅓ cup SPLENDA® No Calorie Sweetener, Granulated

¾ cup 1% low-fat milk

½ cup dried cranberries

½ cup chopped pistachio nuts

1. Preheat oven to 425°F. Spray a cookie sheet with nonstick cooking spray.

2. Combine flour, cream of tartar, baking soda, salt and orange zest in a large bowl; cut in butter with a pastry blender until mixture is crumbly. Add SPLENDA® Granulated Sweetener and milk to dry ingredients, stirring just until dry ingredients are moistened. Stir in cranberries and pistachio nuts.

3. Pat dough to a ¾-inch thickness on a lightly floured surface. Cut scones with a 2½-inch round biscuit cutter and place on cookie sheet.

4. Bake in preheated oven 12 to 15 minutes or until lightly browned.

Makes 14 servings
1 scone

PREP TIME: 10 minutes

COOK TIME: 15 minutes

TOTAL TIME: 25 minutes

Nutrition Information per Serving:
Calories 190 (70 calories from fat), Total Fat 7 g, Saturated Fat 3 g, Protein 4 g, Carbohydrate 26 g, Cholesterol 15 mg, Fiber 2 g, Sodium 230 mg, Sugars 4 g

Blueberry Corn Muffins

- 1¾ cups all-purpose flour
- ½ cup yellow cornmeal
- 1¼ teaspoons baking powder
- ½ teaspoon baking soda
- ½ teaspoon salt
- ¾ cup SPLENDA® No Calorie Sweetener, Granulated
- ½ cup unsalted butter, softened
- ⅓ cup egg substitute
- 2 teaspoons vanilla
- 1 cup buttermilk
- 1 cup blueberries (frozen or fresh)

1. Preheat oven to 350°F. Spray a muffin pan with nonstick cooking spray or line muffin cups with paper liners. Set aside.

2. Blend dry ingredients together in a medium mixing bowl. Set aside.

3. Blend butter in a large mixing bowl until light and fluffy. Add egg substitute slowly. Scrape sides and continue to mix until butter forms small lumps. Add vanilla and buttermilk. Mix well. Add dry ingredients in 3 batches. Mix well and scrape the sides of the bowl after each addition.

4. Fold blueberries gently into batter. Scoop batter into prepared muffin cups, filling cups to the top. Bake in preheated oven 20 to 25 minutes or until done.

Makes 10 servings
1 muffin

PREP TIME: 10 minutes

COOK TIME: 25 minutes

TOTAL TIME: 35 minutes

Nutrition Information per Serving:
Calories 210 (90 calories from fat), Total Fat 10 g, Saturated Fat 6 g, Protein 5 g, Carbohydrate 26 g, Cholesterol 25 mg, Fiber 1 g, Sodium 280 mg, Sugars 2 g

Cheery Cherry Muffins

- ½ **pound fresh or frozen cherries, pitted**
- ¼ **cup margarine**
- ¼ **cup reduced-fat cream cheese**
- ½ **cup SPLENDA® No Calorie Sweetener, Granulated**
- 1 **large egg**
- 2 **cups self-rising flour, sifted**
- 1 **cup nonfat milk**

1. Preheat oven to 400°F. Line a 12-cup muffin tin with paper liners. Lightly spray liners with nonstick cooking spray.

2. Set aside 12 cherries. Chop remaining cherries. Place cherries on a paper towel to drain.

3. Beat margarine and cream cheese at medium speed with an electric mixer until creamy. Add SPLENDA® Granulated Sweetener, beating well. Add egg, beating until blended.

4. Add flour to margarine mixture alternately with milk, beginning and ending with flour. Beat at low speed until blended after each addition. Do not overbeat. Stir in chopped cherries. Spoon 1 tablespoon of batter into each muffin cup. Place a cherry in the center of each cup. Top with remaining batter, filling muffin cups three-fourths full.

5. Bake in preheated oven 25 minutes or until muffins are lightly browned. Remove from pans immediately and cool on wire racks.

Makes 12 *servings*
1 muffin

PREP TIME: 20 minutes

COOK TIME: 25 minutes

TOTAL TIME: 45 minutes

Nutrition Information per Serving:
Calories 150 (50 calories from fat), Total Fat 6 g, Saturated Fat 1 g, Protein 4 g, Carbohydrate 21 g, Cholesterol 20 mg, Fiber 1 g, Sodium 340 mg, Sugars 5 g

Lemon-Orange Walnut Bread

2 cups all-purpose flour

1 teaspoon baking powder

½ teaspoon baking soda

⅔ cup 1% low-fat milk

2 tablespoons lemon juice

1½ teaspoons freshly grated lemon peel

1½ teaspoons freshly grated orange peel

2 large eggs

¾ cup SPLENDA® No Calorie Sweetener, Granulated

½ cup butter, melted

2 teaspoons vanilla extract

¾ cup chopped walnuts

1. Preheat oven to 350°F. Lightly spray an 8½×4½×2½-inch loaf pan with nonstick cooking spray.

2. Combine flour, baking powder and baking soda. Set aside.

3. Combine milk, lemon juice, lemon and orange peels. Set aside.

4. Beat eggs and SPLENDA® Granulated Sweetener on high speed with an electric mixer 5 minutes. Reduce speed to medium; gradually add melted butter and vanilla, beating until blended, about 1 minute.

5. Add flour mixture alternately with milk mixture; beginning and ending with flour mixture. Beat at low speed until blended after each addition. Stir in walnuts. Spoon batter into prepared loaf pan.

6. Bake in preheated oven 30 to 35 minutes or until a long wooden pick inserted in center comes out clean. Cool in pan on a wire rack 10 minutes; remove from pan and cool completely.

Makes 12 servings
1 (½-inch) slice

PREP TIME: 20 minutes

COOK TIME: 35 minutes

TOTAL TIME: 55 minutes

Nutrition Information per Serving:
Calories 220 (120 calories from fat), Total Fat 14 g, Saturated Fat 6 g, Protein 5 g, Carbohydrate 20 g, Cholesterol 55 mg, Fiber 1 g, Sodium 190 mg, Sugars 3 g

Crispy French Toast

- **1 cup 1% low-fat milk**
- **¾ cup half and half**
- **½ cup SPLENDA® No Calorie Sweetener, Granulated**
- **2 tablespoons vanilla extract**
- **4 large eggs**
- **6 thick slices white bread, crusts removed and cut diagonally in half**
- **4 cups cornflakes cereal, finely crushed**
- **2 tablespoons ground cinnamon**
- **1 cup strawberries, sliced**
- **1 cup fat-free vanilla yogurt**
- **Optional Garnish: fresh mint sprigs**

1. Preheat oven to 350°F.

2. Combine milk, half and half, SPLENDA® Granulated Sweetener and vanilla; whisk until SPLENDA® Granulated Sweetener dissolves. Add eggs, whisking until blended.

3. Dip bread into the milk mixture; dredge in cornflakes cereal. Place on a baking sheet.

4. Bake in preheated oven 5 to 10 minutes or until golden brown.

5. Sprinkle a small amount of cinnamon over 6 plates. Arrange 2 toast triangles in the center of each plate. Arrange strawberries around toast; top toast with a small scoop of vanilla yogurt. Sprinkle with cinnamon. Garnish with fresh mint sprigs, if desired.

Makes 6 servings
1 slice French toast, 3 tablespoons strawberries, 3 tablespoons yogurt

PREP TIME: 10 minutes

COOK TIME: 10 minutes

TOTAL TIME: 20 minutes

Nutrition Information per Serving:
Calories 320 (80 calories from fat), Total Fat 9 g, Saturated Fat 4 g, Protein 12 g, Carbohydrate 44 g, Cholesterol 155 mg, Fiber 3 g, Sodium 460 mg, Sugars 10 g

Cinnamon-Pecan Monkey Bread

¼ **cup chopped pecans**

2 **tablespoons butter**

¼ **cup SPLENDA® Brown Sugar Blend**

¼ **teaspoon ground cinnamon**

⅓ **cup SPLENDA® Brown Sugar Blend**

¼ **teaspoon ground cinnamon**

½ **(3-pound) package frozen roll dough, thawed**

3 **tablespoons butter, melted**

1. Spray a 12-cup bundt pan with nonstick cooking spray. Sprinkle pecans in bottom of pan; set aside.

2. Combine 2 tablespoons butter, ¼ cup SPLENDA® Brown Sugar Blend and ¼ teaspoon cinnamon in a small saucepan; cook over low heat, stirring constantly until blended; pour mixture over pecans. Set aside.

3. Combine ⅓ cup SPLENDA® Brown Sugar Blend and ¼ teaspoon cinnamon in a small bowl; set aside.

4. Cut each roll into half; dip tops of balls into melted butter and then into SPLENDA® Brown Sugar Blend mixture. Place in prepared pan. (At this point Monkey Bread may be covered and stored in the refrigerator 8 hours or overnight, or proceed as directed). Cover and let rise in a warm place, free from drafts, 50 minutes or until doubled in bulk.

5. Preheat oven to 350°F about 10 minutes prior to baking. Bake 25 to 30 minutes or until bread sounds hollow when tapped. Remove from pan; cool on a wire rack. Serve warm.

Makes 18 servings
1 slice (1/18 of monkey bread)

PREP TIME: 20 minutes

COOK TIME: 25 minutes

TOTAL TIME: 1 hour, 35 minutes

Nutrition Information per Serving:
Calories 180 (60 calories from fat), Total Fat 6 g, Saturated Fat 2 g, Protein 4 g, Carbohydrate 24 g, Cholesterol 10 mg, Fiber 1 g, Sodium 290 mg, Sugars 9 g

Pumpkin Waffles

1 **cup all-purpose flour**

1 **teaspoon baking powder**

½ **teaspoon baking soda**

¼ **teaspoon salt**

¾ **teaspoon ground cinnamon**

½ **teaspoon ground ginger**

⅛ **teaspoon ground nutmeg**

2 **teaspoons canola oil**

1 **teaspoon molasses**

¼ **cup canned pumpkin**

1 **cup buttermilk**

1 **large egg**

2 **tablespoons SPLENDA® No Calorie Sweetener, Granulated**

1½ **cups maple syrup sweetened with SPLENDA® Brand Sweetener**

1. Preheat waffle iron according to manufacturer's directions; spray lightly with nonstick cooking spray.

2. Combine flour, baking powder, baking soda, salt, cinnamon, ginger and nutmeg in a large bowl. Set aside.

3. Combine oil, molasses, pumpkin and buttermilk in a small bowl. Set aside.

4. Whisk together egg and SPLENDA® Granulated Sweetener until blended. Add buttermilk mixture, whisking until blended. Add to dry ingredients, stirring just until moistened.

5. Pour batter into hot waffle iron and bake approximately 5 minutes. Serve with maple syrup.

Makes 6 servings
1 waffle

PREP TIME: 15 minutes

COOK TIME: 5 minutes

TOTAL TIME: 20 minutes

Nutrition Information per Serving:
Calories 160 (25 calories from fat), Total Fat 3 g, Saturated Fat 1 g, Protein 5 g, Carbohydrate 32 g, Cholesterol 35 mg, Fiber 1 g, Sodium 400 mg, Sugars 3 g

Main Dishes & Sides

Raspberry Cocktail Sauce with Chilled Shrimp

Cocktail Sauce:

- 1 **cup no-sugar-added raspberry preserves**
- ¼ **cup prepared horseradish**
- 3 **tablespoons SPLENDA® No Calorie Sweetener, Granulated**
- 2 **tablespoons tomato paste**
- 3 **teaspoons sherry wine vinegar**
- 2 **tablespoons Worcestershire sauce**
- 1 **clove garlic, minced**
- 1 **jalapeño pepper, minced**
- ½ **teaspoon salt**
- 1 **pinch black pepper**

- 2 **pounds cooked, peeled and deveined shrimp**

1. Place cocktail sauce ingredients in a food processor or a blender. Process or blend for 30 seconds or until smooth.

2. Chill cocktail sauce at least 2 hours before serving. Serve with shrimp. Cocktail sauce will keep, refrigerated, for 5 days.

Makes 32 servings
2 shrimp, 1 tablespoon sauce

PREP TIME: 5 minutes

TOTAL TIME: 2 hours, 5 minutes

Nutrition Information per Serving:
Calories 45 (0 calories from fat), Total Fat 0 g, Saturated Fat 0 g, Protein 6 g, Carbohydrate 4 g, Cholesterol 55 mg, Fiber 1 g, Sodium 125 mg, Sugars 3 g

Cucumber and Onion Salad

2½ cups thinly sliced unpeeled cucumbers

½ cup thinly sliced red onions

⅓ cup SPLENDA® No Calorie Sweetener, Granulated

⅓ cup white vinegar

¼ teaspoon salt

⅛ teaspoon black pepper

1. Place cucumbers and onions in a non-metallic medium bowl.

2. Combine remaining ingredients in a small mixing bowl. Stir well. Pour over cucumbers and onions. Cover and refrigerate for at least 2 hours. Stir occasionally.

Makes 6 servings
¾ cup salad

PREP TIME: 15 minutes
TOTAL TIME: 2 hours, 15 minutes

Nutrition Information per Serving:
Calories 15 (0 calories from fat), Total Fat 0 g, Saturated Fat 0 g, Protein 1 g, Carbohydrate 3 g, Cholesterol 0 mg, Fiber 1 g, Sodium 100 mg, Sugars 2 g

Boston-Style Baked Beans

4 (15-ounce) cans navy beans

½ pound bacon, chopped

1 medium onion, chopped

¼ cup yellow mustard

⅓ cup **SPLENDA® No Calorie Sweetener, Granulated**

2 tablespoons robust molasses

Makes 18 servings
½ cup

PREP TIME: 15 minutes

COOK TIME: 45 minutes

TOTAL TIME: 1 hour

Nutrition Information per Serving:
Calories 140 (25 calories from fat), Total Fat 3 g, Saturated Fat 1 g, Protein 9 g, Carbohydrate 21 g, Cholesterol 5 mg, Fiber 5 g, Sodium 520 mg, Sugars 3 g

1. Preheat oven to 350°F.

2. Drain navy beans and reserve 1¼ cups liquid.

3. Cook bacon in a large skillet until browned. Remove bacon and reserve half of the bacon fat.

4. Cook onion in reserved bacon fat and cook until translucent. Stir in beans and remaining ingredients.

5. Pour beans into a 3-quart baking dish. Bake in preheated oven 45 minutes.

Lemon Glazed Jumbo Shrimp Salad

1 tablespoon extra-virgin olive oil

8 jumbo shrimp, peeled and deveined

½ cup fresh lemon juice

½ cup cider vinegar

½ cup SPLENDA® No Calorie Sweetener, Granulated

½ teaspoon crushed red pepper

1 jalapeño, trimmed, seeded and thinly sliced

2 cups baby arugula leaves

½ cup thinly sliced red bell pepper

½ cup thinly sliced mango

Salt and pepper to taste

1. Heat oil in a medium skillet over high heat; add shrimp and cook 1 minute. Stir in lemon juice and cook 3 to 4 minutes or until shrimp are cooked through. Using tongs, transfer shrimp to a plate. Add vinegar, SPLENDA® Granulated Sweetener, crushed red pepper and jalapeño; bring to a boil and cook 4 to 5 minutes or until reduced by half, then remove from heat and set aside.

2. Place arugula, red pepper and mango in a large bowl; toss gently with some of the dressing and season to taste.

3. Divide arugula mixture among 4 serving plates; top each salad with 2 shrimp and drizzle evenly with the warm vinegar mixture.

Makes 4 servings
2 jumbo shrimp, ¾ cup salad

PREP TIME: 10 minutes

COOK TIME: 12 minutes

TOTAL TIME: 22 minutes

Nutrition Information per Serving:
Calories 120 (40 calories from fat), Total Fat 4 g, Saturated Fat 1 g, Protein 12 g, Carbohydrate 10 g, Cholesterol 105 mg, Fiber 1 g, Sodium 220 mg, Sugars 6 g

Chicken Cacciatore over Pasta

1 pound boneless, skinless chicken breast halves

½ cup chopped onion

½ cup chopped green bell pepper

1 (16-ounce) can chopped tomatoes, drained

1 (8-ounce) can tomato sauce

2 tablespoons SPLENDA® No Calorie Sweetener, Granulated

1½ teaspoons Italian seasoning

⅓ cup sliced ripe olives

⅛ teaspoon black pepper

3 cups hot cooked noodles (or any favorite pasta), rinsed and drained

1. Slice chicken breasts into 32 pieces.

2. Spray a large skillet with olive oil-flavored nonstick cooking spray. Sauté chicken, onion and green pepper for 6 to 8 minutes. Stir in drained tomatoes and tomato sauce.

3. Add SPLENDA® Granulated Sweetener, Italian seasoning, olives and black pepper. Mix well to combine. Lower heat and simmer for 10 to 15 minutes, stirring occasionally.

4. For each serving, place ½ cup pasta on a plate and spoon ⅔ cup chicken and sauce mixture over top.

Makes 6 servings
½ cup noodles, ¾ cup chicken cacciatore

PREP TIME: 10 minutes

COOK TIME: 23 minutes

TOTAL TIME: 33 minutes

Nutrition Information per Serving:
Calories 210 (40 calories from fat), Total Fat 4 g, Saturated Fat 1 g, Protein 21 g, Carbohydrate 22 g, Cholesterol 65 mg, Fiber 3 g, Sodium 460 mg, Sugars 5 g

Easy Lemon Chicken

1 teaspoon cornstarch

1 tablespoon low-sodium soy sauce

12 ounces chicken breast tenders, cut into thirds

¼ cup fresh lemon juice

¼ cup low-sodium soy sauce

¼ cup fat-free chicken broth

1 teaspoon fresh ginger, minced

2 cloves garlic, minced

1 tablespoon SPLENDA® No Calorie Sweetener, Granulated

1 teaspoon cornstarch

1 tablespoon vegetable oil

¼ cup red bell pepper, sliced into 2-inch strips

¼ cup green bell pepper, sliced into 2-inch strips

1. Mix 1 teaspoon cornstarch and 1 tablespoon soy sauce in a small mixing bowl. Add sliced chicken tenders. Place in refrigerator and marinate for 10 minutes.

2. Stir the lemon juice, ¼ cup soy sauce, chicken broth, ginger, garlic, SPLENDA® Granulated Sweetener and 1 teaspoon cornstarch together in a medium mixing bowl.

3. Heat oil in a medium skillet. Add chicken and cook over medium-high heat 3 to 4 minutes or until just done. Add sauce and sliced peppers. Cook 1 to 2 minutes more or until sauce thickens and peppers are slightly tender.

Makes 4 servings
¾ cup lemon chicken

PREP TIME: 10 minutes

COOK TIME: 10 minutes

TOTAL TIME: 20 minutes

Nutrition Information per Serving:
Calories 150 (40 calories from fat), Total Fat 5 g, Saturated Fat 1 g, Protein 21 g, Carbohydrate 6 g, Cholesterol 50 mg, Fiber 1 g, Sodium 730 mg, Sugars 1 g

Polynesian Pork Chops

½ **cup vegetable oil**

6 **lean pork chops**

2 **large eggs**

1 **cup all-purpose flour**

1 **(29-ounce) can diced peaches with heavy syrup**

½ **cup SPLENDA® Brown Sugar Blend**

½ **cup water, or as needed**

1. Heat oil in a skillet over medium heat.

2. Clean and de-bone the pork chops. In a small bowl, whisk eggs and set aside. In another bowl, add flour and any additional spices, if desired. Dip pork chops in egg and then flour.

3. Place the coated pork chops into the skillet.

4. Cook for 25 minutes, turning as needed.

5. Turn the heat to low; add peaches and SPLENDA® Brown Sugar Blend to the skillet on top of the pork chops. Add water if the chops look too dry.

6. Simmer for 10 minutes and serve.

Makes 6 servings
1 pork chop, ½ cup diced peach sauce

PREP TIME: 2 minutes

COOK TIME: 35 minutes

TOTAL TIME: 37 minutes

Nutrition Information per Serving:
Calories 590 (240 calories from fat), Total Fat 27 g, Saturated Fat 6 g, Protein 34 g, Carbohydrate 48 g, Cholesterol 145 mg, Fiber 2 g, Sodium 85 mg, Sugars 30 g

Fluffy Carrot Soufflé

1 **pound baby carrots**

2 **cups water**

½ **teaspoon salt**

¼ **cup butter**

3 **tablespoons all-purpose flour**

1 **teaspoon baking powder**

¼ **cup SPLENDA® No Calorie Sweetener, Granulated**

3 **large eggs**

1 **teaspoon vanilla extract**

1. Preheat oven to 350°F.

2. Combine carrots, water and salt in a medium saucepan; bring to a boil. Reduce heat and cook, covered, 12 to 15 minutes or until carrots are tender. Drain.

3. Process carrots and butter in a food processor until smooth, stopping once to scrape down sides.

4. Combine flour, baking powder and SPLENDA® Granulated Sweetener, add to carrot mixture and process until blended. Add eggs, one at a time, and process until blended. Add vanilla and pulse 2 or 3 times.

5. Spoon mixture into a greased 1-quart baking dish.

6. Bake in preheated oven 30 to 45 minutes or until thoroughly heated.

7. Serve immediately.

Makes 5 servings
½ cup soufflé

PREP TIME: 30 minutes

COOK TIME: 45 minutes

TOTAL TIME: 1 hour, 15 minutes

Nutrition Information per Serving:
Calories 180 (120 calories from fat), Total Fat 13 g, Saturated Fat 7 g, Protein 5 g, Carbohydrate 13 g, Cholesterol 150 mg, Fiber 2 g, Sodium 450 mg, Sugars 6 g

Sweet Potato Casserole

4 **medium sweet potatoes**

¾ **cup SPLENDA® No Calorie Sweetener, Granulated**

½ **cup whole milk**

2 **teaspoons grated orange zest**

¼ **cup fresh orange juice**

2 **teaspoons vanilla extract**

1 **large egg, lightly beaten**

½ **cup all-purpose flour**

3 **tablespoons butter, melted**

1 **cup panko bread crumbs**

½ **cup finely chopped pecans**

2 **tablespoons butter, melted**

3 **tablespoons maple syrup**

1. Preheat oven to 375°F. Lightly grease a 13×9-inch baking dish.

2. Place sweet potatoes on a baking sheet; bake in preheated oven 1 hour or until done. Cool to touch. Peel and mash. Reduce oven to 350°F.

3. Combine sweet potatoes and next 8 ingredients in a large bowl. Beat at medium speed with an electric mixer until smooth. Spoon into baking dish.

4. Combine panko and remaining ingredients; sprinkle crumb mixture over top of casserole. Bake an additional 1 hour or until casserole is thoroughly heated.

Makes 14 servings
½ cup sweet potato casserole

PREP TIME: 10 minutes

COOK TIME: 2 hours

TOTAL TIME: 2 hours, 10 minutes

Nutrition Information per Serving:
Calories 190 (70 calories from fat), Total Fat 8 g, Saturated Fat 3 g, Protein 4 g, Carbohydrate 29 g, Cholesterol 30 mg, Fiber 3 g, Sodium 95 mg, Sugars 10 g

Sensational Pumpkin Bake

2 **(15-ounce) cans 100% pure pumpkin**

4 **tablespoons SPLENDA® Brown Sugar Blend, divided**

¼ **cup butter or margarine**

¼ **teaspoon ground cinnamon**

⅛ **teaspoon ground nutmeg**

¼ **cup chopped pecans, toasted**

1. Preheat oven to 350°F.

2. Combine pumpkin, 3 tablespoons of the SPLENDA® Brown Sugar Blend, butter, cinnamon and nutmeg in medium saucepan. Cook over medium heat, stirring occasionally, until mixture comes to a boil. Reduce heat to low; cook 1 to 2 minutes.

Pour hot mixture into an ungreased 1½-quart casserole dish. Combine remaining 1 tablespoon of the SPLENDA® Brown Sugar Blend and pecans in small bowl. Sprinkle over pumpkin.

3. Bake in preheated oven 5 to 10 minutes or until browned.

Makes 8 servings
½ cup pumpkin bake

PREP TIME: 15 minutes

COOK TIME: 10 minutes

TOTAL TIME: 25 minutes

Nutrition Information per Serving:
Calories 150 (80 calories from fat), Total Fat 9 g, Saturated Fat 4 g, Protein 2 g, Carbohydrate 17 g, Cholesterol 15 mg, Fiber 3 g, Sodium 320 mg, Sugars 11 g

Cookies & Bites

Tangy Coconut Tartlets

1½ cups sweetened flaked coconut

¼ cup **SPLENDA® No Calorie Sweetener, Granulated**

¾ cup all-purpose flour

2 teaspoons vanilla extract

2 egg whites

1 (3.4-ounce) package instant lemon pudding mix

2 cups nonfat milk

1 (8-ounce) container fat-free frozen whipped topping, thawed

1 tablespoon unsweetened flaked coconut, toasted

1. Preheat oven to 400°F. Lightly grease 24 mini-muffin cups.

2. In a mixing bowl, combine 1½ cups coconut, SPLENDA® Granulated Sweetener, flour, vanilla and egg whites; stir well. Divide mixture evenly among the prepared mini-muffin cups, pressing mixture into bottom and up sides of muffin cups.

3. Bake in preheated oven until the edges are browned. Cool 2 minutes in the muffin tins on a wire rack. Remove from tins and cool completely on a wire rack.

4. Prepare lemon pudding according to package instructions using the milk. Spoon lemon mixture into each macaroon tartlet shell. Top with 2 teaspoons of whipped topping sprinkled with a pinch of toasted coconut.

Makes 24 servings
1 tartlet

PREP TIME: 20 minutes

COOK TIME: 20 minutes

TOTAL TIME: 40 minutes

Nutrition Information per Serving:
Calories 80 (15 calories from fat), Total Fat 2 g, Saturated Fat 1 g, Protein 2 g, Carbohydrate 13 g, Cholesterol 0 mg, Fiber 0 g, Sodium 85 mg, Sugars 7 g

Old Fashioned Peanut Butter Chocolate Chip Cookies

1½ cups all-purpose flour

1 teaspoon baking soda

1 cup butter or margarine, softened

½ cup creamy or chunky peanut butter

½ cup SPLENDA® Sugar Blend

½ cup SPLENDA® Brown Sugar Blend, packed

1 teaspoon vanilla extract

1 large egg

1⅓ cups NESTLÉ® TOLL HOUSE® Peanut Butter & Milk Chocolate Morsels

1. Preheat oven to 375°F.

2. Combine flour and baking soda in small bowl. Set aside.

3. Beat butter, peanut butter, SPLENDA® Sugar Blend, SPLENDA® Brown Sugar Blend and vanilla in large bowl until creamy. Beat in egg. Gradually beat in flour mixture. Stir in morsels.

4. Drop dough by rounded tablespoons onto ungreased baking sheets. Press down slightly with bottom of glass dipped in SPLENDA® Sugar Blend.

5. Bake in preheated oven 8 to 10 minutes or until edges are set but centers are still soft. Cool on baking sheets 4 minutes. Remove to wire racks to cool completely.

Makes 36 servings
1 cookie

PREP TIME: 10 minutes

COOK TIME: 10 minutes

TOTAL TIME: 20 minutes

Nutrition Information per Serving:
Calories 120 (70 calories from fat), Total Fat 7 g, Saturated Fat 4 g, Protein 2 g, Carbohydrate 11 g, Cholesterol 20 mg, Fiber 0 g, Sodium 105 mg, Sugars 7 g

Merry Gingerbread Cookies

6 cups all-purpose flour

1 teaspoon baking soda

½ teaspoon baking powder

4 teaspoons ground ginger

4 teaspoons ground cinnamon

1½ teaspoons ground cloves

1 cup unsalted butter, softened

1 cup SPLENDA® No Calorie Sweetener, Granulated

1 teaspoon salt

2 large eggs

1 cup molasses

3 tablespoons water

1. Blend together flour, baking soda, baking powder and spices in a large mixing bowl.

2. Cream butter, SPLENDA® Granulated Sweetener and salt together in a large mixing bowl. Add eggs, one at a time, beating well after each addition. Add molasses and water. Stir well. Add flour mixture and stir until well blended. Refrigerate dough 1 to 2 hours before rolling out and cutting into shapes.

3. Preheat oven to 350°F. Roll cookie dough out slightly less than ¼-inch thick. Cut into desired shapes. Bake in preheated oven 8 to 10 minutes or until lightly browned on the bottom.

Makes 54 servings
1 cookie

PREP TIME: 30 minutes

COOK TIME: 10 minutes

TOTAL TIME: 1 hour, 40 minutes

Nutrition Information per Serving:
Calories 100 (35 calories from fat), Total Fat 4 g, Saturated Fat 2 g, Protein 2 g, Carbohydrate 15 g, Cholesterol 15 mg, Fiber 1 g, Sodium 75 mg, Sugars 4 g

Sand Tarts

1 cup butter, softened

¼ cup SPLENDA® No Calorie Sweetener, Granulated

2 cups all-purpose flour

2 teaspoons vanilla extract

1 cup chopped pecans

2 tablespoons SPLENDA® No Calorie Sweetener, Granulated

2 teaspoons cornstarch

1. Preheat oven to 350°F.

2. Beat butter and ¼ cup SPLENDA® Granulated Sweetener at medium speed with an electric mixer about 2 minutes or until creamy. Gradually add flour, beating at low speed until blended. Stir in vanilla and pecans. Shape into 1-inch balls.

3. Bake in preheated oven 20 minutes; remove from oven and place on wire racks to cool.

4. Process 2 tablespoons SPLENDA® Granulated Sweetener and cornstarch in a blender or food processor; roll cookies in powdered SPLENDA® Granulated Sweetener mixture.

Makes 42 servings
1 cookie

PREP TIME: 15 minutes

COOK TIME: 20 minutes

TOTAL TIME: 35 minutes

Nutrition Information per Serving:
Calories 80 (60 calories from fat), Total Fat 6 g, Saturated Fat 3 g, Protein 1 g, Carbohydrate 5 g, Cholesterol 10 mg, Fiber 0 g, Sodium 45 mg, Sugars 0 g

Almond Cheesecake Bars

Crust:

¼ cup SPLENDA® No Calorie Sweetener, Granulated

1¼ cups graham cracker or vanilla wafer crumbs

⅓ cup light butter, melted

¼ cup toasted sliced almonds, finely ground

Filling:

12 ounces reduced-fat cream cheese

½ cup SPLENDA® No Calorie Sweetener, Granulated

2 large eggs

¼ cup reduced-fat sour cream

2½ teaspoons vanilla extract

1 teaspoon almond extract

¼ cup toasted, sliced almonds

1. Preheat oven to 350°F. Spray an 8-inch square baking pan with nonstick cooking spray. Set aside.

2. Prepare Crust. Mix crust ingredients together in a mixing bowl. Mix well. Press into prepared pan. Bake 10 to 12 minutes or until firm.

3. Prepare Filling. Mix cream cheese and SPLENDA® Granulated Sweetener together until smooth. Add eggs, one at a time, scraping the sides of the bowl and mixing well after each addition. Add sour cream and extracts; mix well. Pour over prepared crust.

4. Bake in preheated oven 40 to 47 minutes or until firm.

5. Top with toasted almonds.

Makes 20 servings

1 (1.6-inch × 2-inch) bar

PREP TIME: 15 minutes

COOK TIME: 59 minutes

TOTAL TIME: 1 hour, 14 minutes

Nutrition Information per Serving:
Calories 110 (70 calories from fat), Total Fat 8 g, Saturated Fat 4 g, Protein 4 g, Carbohydrate 7 g, Cholesterol 35 mg, Fiber 0 g, Sodium 105 mg, Sugars 3 g

After-School Butterscotch Brownies

2¼ cups all-purpose flour

1 teaspoon baking powder

½ teaspoon salt

1 cup butter or margarine, softened

¾ cup SPLENDA® Brown Sugar Blend, packed

1 tablespoon vanilla extract

2 large eggs

1 (11-ounce package) NESTLÉ® TOLL HOUSE® Butterscotch Flavored Morsels, divided

½ cup chopped pecans

1. Preheat oven to 350°F.

2. Combine flour, baking powder and salt in medium bowl. Set aside.

3. Combine butter, SPLENDA® Brown Sugar Blend and vanilla in a large mixing bowl; beat at medium speed until creamy. Beat in eggs. Gradually beat in flour mixture. Stir in 1 cup morsels and pecans. Spread into an ungreased 13×9-inch baking pan. Sprinkle with remaining ⅔ cup morsels.

4. Bake in preheated oven 30 to 40 minutes or until wooden pick inserted in center comes out clean. Cool in pan on wire rack. Cut into bars.

Makes 48 servings
1 (1.5-inch-square) bar

PREP TIME: 10 minutes

COOK TIME: 30 minutes

TOTAL TIME: 40 minutes

Nutrition Information per Serving:
Calories 120 (60 calories from fat), Total Fat 7 g, Saturated Fat 4 g, Protein 1 g, Carbohydrate 12 g, Cholesterol 20 mg, Fiber 0 g, Sodium 75 mg, Sugars 7 g

Oat-Date Bars

8 **ounces chopped dates**

¾ **cup NESTLÉ® CARNATION® Lowfat 2% Evaporated Milk**

1 **tablespoon SPLENDA® Sugar Blend**

1 **teaspoon vanilla extract**

1 **cup all-purpose flour**

¾ **cup quick-cooking oats**

½ **teaspoon baking soda**

½ **teaspoon salt**

½ **teaspoon ground cinnamon**

½ **cup butter or margarine, softened**

¼ **cup SPLENDA® Brown Sugar Blend, packed**

1. Preheat oven to 400°F. Spray an 8-inch square baking pan with nonstick cooking spray.

2. Combine dates, evaporated milk, SPLENDA® Sugar Blend and vanilla in medium saucepan. Cook on medium-low heat, stirring occasionally, 8 to 10 minutes or until thickened. Remove from heat.

3. Combine flour, oats, baking soda, salt and cinnamon in a medium bowl. Set aside.

4. Combine butter and SPLENDA® Brown Sugar Blend in large bowl; beat at medium speed until creamy. Beat in flour mixture. With floured fingers, press half of crust mixture onto bottom of prepared baking pan. Spread date filling over crust. Top with remaining crust mixture.

5. Bake in preheated oven 20 to 25 minutes or until golden. Cut into bars. Serve warm.

Makes 16 servings
1 (2-inch square) bar

PREP TIME: 15 minutes

COOK TIME: 20 minutes

TOTAL TIME: 35 minutes

Nutrition Information per Serving:
Calories 160 (60 calories from fat), Total Fat 6 g, Saturated Fat 4 g, Protein 3 g, Carbohydrate 24 g, Cholesterol 20 mg, Fiber 2 g, Sodium 190 mg, Sugars 14 g

Coconut-Date-Nut Balls

¾ **cup flaked coconut**

½ **cup butter**

1 **(8-ounce) package dates, chopped**

¾ **cup chopped pecans**

½ **cup egg substitute**

¾ **cup SPLENDA® No Calorie Sweetener, Granulated**

3½ **cups crispy rice cereal**

1. Preheat oven to 350°F. Bake coconut, stirring occasionally, 5 to 6 minutes or until toasted. Set aside.

2. Melt butter in a large skillet over low heat. Add dates and pecans; cook over low heat, stirring constantly until dates are softened. Cool to touch (about 5 minutes).

3. Beat egg substitute and SPLENDA® Granulated Sweetener for 3 minutes at medium speed with an electric mixer; add to date mixture. Cook over low heat, stirring constantly, until mixture thickens (about 3 minutes). Stir in rice cereal. Cool to touch. Shape into 1-inch balls. Roll in toasted coconut.

Makes 36 servings
1 ball

PREP TIME: 10 minutes

COOK TIME: 14 minutes

TOTAL TIME: 24 minutes

Nutrition Information per Serving:
Calories 80 (45 calories from fat), Total Fat 5 g, Saturated Fat 2 g, Protein 1 g, Carbohydrate 8 g, Cholesterol 5 mg, Fiber 1 g, Sodium 55 mg, Sugars 5 g

Peanut Butter and Jelly Bites

Peanut Butter Balls:

- 1 **stick SPLENDA® No Calorie Sweetener Flavors for Coffee, Caramel**
- 1 **stick SPLENDA® No Calorie Sweetener Flavors for Coffee, French Vanilla**
- 1 **tablespoon sugar-free cocoa mix**
- 1 **tablespoon graham cracker crumbs**
- 2 **tablespoons peanut butter**
- 1½ **teaspoons fat-free cream cheese**

Garnish:

- 2 **tablespoons graham cracker crumbs**
- 2 **teaspoons sugar-free or no-sugar-added jam**

1. Mix all peanut butter ball ingredients together in a small bowl. Roll into 6 balls. Roll balls in graham cracker crumbs.

2. Press a small indentation in center with fingertip. Fill with jam. Serve immediately.

Makes 2 servings
3 prepared bites

PREP TIME: 10 minutes

TOTAL TIME: 10 minutes

Nutrition Information per Serving:
Calories 150 (80 calories from fat), Total Fat 9 g, Saturated Fat 2 g, Protein 6 g, Carbohydrate 15 g, Cholesterol 0 mg, Fiber 1 g, Sodium 170 mg, Sugars 5 g

Peanut Butter Cookie Bites

¼ **cup margarine, softened**

1 **cup creamy peanut butter**

¼ **cup egg substitute**

2 **tablespoons honey**

½ **teaspoon vanilla extract**

1 **cup SPLENDA® No Calorie Sweetener, Granulated**

1½ **cups all-purpose flour**

½ **teaspoon baking soda**

½ **teaspoon salt**

1. Preheat oven to 350°F.

2. Beat margarine and peanut butter in a large mixing bowl with an electric mixer until creamy, approximately 1 minute.

3. Add egg substitute, honey and vanilla. Beat on high speed for approximately 1½ minutes.

4. Add SPLENDA® Granulated Sweetener and beat on medium speed until well blended, approximately 30 seconds.

5. Combine flour, baking soda and salt in a small mixing bowl. Slowly add flour mixture to peanut butter mixture, beating on low speed until well blended, about 1½ minutes. Mixture may be crumbly.

6. Roll level tablespoons of dough into balls and drop onto a lightly oiled or parchment-lined cookie sheet, 2 inches apart. Flatten each ball with a fork, pressing a crisscross pattern into each cookie. Bake in preheated oven 7 to 9 minutes or until light brown around the edges. Cool on wire rack.

Makes 24 servings
1 prepared bite

PREP TIME: 20 minutes

COOK TIME: 9 minutes

TOTAL TIME: 29 minutes

Nutrition Information per Serving:
Calories 120 (70 calories from fat), Total Fat 8 g, Saturated Fat 1 g, Protein 4 g, Carbohydrate 10 g, Cholesterol 0 mg, Fiber 1 g, Sodium 150 mg, Sugars 2 g

Pies & Desserts

S'mores Campfire Pie

Filling:

- ½ cup SPLENDA® Sugar Blend
- ⅓ cup fat-free half and half
- 1 teaspoon vanilla extract
- 4 (1-ounce) squares unsweetened chocolate, chopped
- 1 (9-inch) graham cracker crust

Meringue:

- 4 egg whites
- ¼ teaspoon cream of tartar
- 1 teaspoon vanilla extract
- ½ cup SPLENDA® Sugar Blend

1. Prepare Filling. Combine SPLENDA® Sugar Blend and half and half in a small saucepan. Cook over medium heat, stirring constantly, until SPLENDA® Sugar Blend dissolves. Stir in vanilla; add chocolate, stirring until chocolate melts. Pour mixture into crust. Set aside.

2. Preheat oven to 225°F.

3. Prepare Meringue. Combine egg whites, cream of tartar and vanilla in a large mixing bowl; beat at high speed with an electric mixer until foamy. Gradually add SPLENDA® Sugar Blend, 1 tablespoon at a time, beating until stiff peaks form and SPLENDA® Sugar Blend dissolves. Spread meringue evenly over chocolate filling.

4. Bake in preheated oven 2 hours. Turn oven off and leave in oven, with door closed and oven light on, for 8 hours or overnight.

Makes 8 servings
1 slice (⅛ pie)

PREP TIME: 15 minutes

COOK TIME: 2 hours

TOTAL TIME: 10 hours, 15 minutes

Nutrition Information per Serving:
Calories 340 (130 calories from fat), Total Fat 14 g, Saturated Fat 6 g, Protein 5 g, Carbohydrate 46 g, Cholesterol 0 mg, Fiber 3 g, Sodium 190 mg, Sugars 37 g

Apple Cranberry Pie

1 **(15-ounce) package refrigerated pie crusts**

½ **cup SPLENDA® No Calorie Sweetener, Granulated**

1 **tablespoon all-purpose flour**

½ **teaspoon ground cinnamon**

4 **large Granny Smith apples, peeled, cored and sliced**

1 **cup cranberries, coarsely chopped**

1. Preheat oven to 400°F.

2. Unfold 1 pie crust; press out fold lines. Fit pie crust into a 9-inch pie plate according to package directions.

3. Combine SPLENDA® Granulated Sweetener, flour and cinnamon in a large bowl; add apples and cranberries, tossing gently. Spoon mixture into pie crust.

4. Unfold remaining pie crust; press out fold lines. Roll to ⅛-inch thickness. Place over filling; fold edges under and crimp. Cut slits in top to allow steam to escape.

5. Bake 40 to 50 minutes or until crust is golden. Cover edges with aluminum foil to prevent overbrowning, if necessary. Cool on a wire rack 1 hour before serving.

Makes 8 servings
1 slice (⅛ pie)

PREP TIME: 30 minutes

COOK TIME: 50 minutes

TOTAL TIME: 1 hour, 20 minutes

Nutrition Information per Serving:
Calories 290 (130 calories from fat), Total Fat 14 g, Saturated Fat 6 g, Protein 2 g, Carbohydrate 41 g, Cholesterol 10 mg, Fiber 3 g, Sodium 200 mg, Sugars 13 g

Nostalgic Apple Pie

1 **(15-ounce) package refrigerated pie crusts**

7 **cups baking apples, peeled, cored and thinly sliced**

1 **cup SPLENDA® No Calorie Sweetener, Granulated**

3 **tablespoons cornstarch**

¾ **teaspoon ground cinnamon**

¼ **teaspoon ground nutmeg**

⅛ **teaspoon salt**

1. Preheat oven to 425°F.

2. Unfold 1 pie crust; press out fold lines. Fit pie crust into a 9-inch pie plate according to package directions.

3. Place sliced apples into a large mixing bowl; set aside. Combine SPLENDA® Granulated Sweetener, cornstarch, cinnamon, nutmeg and salt in a small bowl. Sprinkle mixture over apples and toss. Spoon apple mixture into pie crust. Place the second crust over the filling. Seal edges, trim and flute. Cut small slits in top to allow steam to escape.

4. Bake in preheated oven 40 to 50 minutes or until the crust is golden. Serve warm or chilled.

Makes 8 servings
1 slice (⅛ pie)

PREP TIME: 15 minutes

COOK TIME: 50 minutes

TOTAL TIME: 1 hour, 5 minutes

Nutrition Information per Serving:
Calories 300 (140 calories from fat), Total Fat 15 g, Saturated Fat 4 g, Protein 3 g, Carbohydrate 40 g, Cholesterol 0 mg, Fiber 5 g, Sodium 270 mg, Sugars 14 g

Berry-Cherry Pie

1 **(15-ounce) package refrigerated pie crusts**

1 **(14.5-ounce) can pitted tart red cherries, undrained**

1 **(12-ounce) package frozen raspberries, thawed**

1 **cup fresh blueberries or frozen blueberries, thawed**

1 **cup SPLENDA® No Calorie Sweetener, Granulated**

¼ **cup cornstarch**

2 **tablespoons butter**

Optional topping: frozen low-fat vanilla yogurt

1. Preheat oven to 375°F.

2. Unfold 1 pie crust; press out fold lines. Fit pie crust into a 9-inch pie plate according to package directions.

3. Drain cherries, raspberries and blueberries (if frozen), reserving 1 cup of the juices. Set berries and juice aside.

4. Combine SPLENDA® Granulated Sweetener and cornstarch in a medium saucepan; gradually stir in reserved juice. Cook over medium heat, stirring constantly until mixture begins to boil. Boil 1 minute, stirring constantly. Stir in butter and reserved fruit. Cool slightly and spoon mixture into pie shell.

5. Unroll remaining pie crust; roll to ⅛-inch thickness. Place over filling. Seal edges, trim and flute. Cut slits in top to allow steam to escape.

6. Bake in preheated oven 40 to 45 minutes or until crust is golden. Cover edges with aluminum foil to prevent overbrowning, if necessary. Cool on a wire rack. Serve with a scoop of frozen yogurt, if desired.

Makes 8 servings
1 slice (⅛ pie)

PREP TIME: 25 minutes

COOK TIME: 45 minutes

TOTAL TIME: 1 hour, 10 minutes

Nutrition Information per Serving:
Calories 330 (170 calories from fat), Total Fat 19 g, Saturated Fat 6 g, Protein 4 g, Carbohydrate 37 g, Cholesterol 10 mg, Fiber 4 g, Sodium 290 mg, Sugars 7 g

Chocolate Velvet Mousse

- 3 ounces unsweetened chocolate
- 1 cup 1% low-fat milk
- ¼ cup egg substitute
- ½ cup SPLENDA® No Calorie Sweetener, Granulated
- 1 teaspoon cornstarch
- 2 tablespoons orange-flavored liqueur or brandy*
- ½ cup heavy cream
- 3 cups sliced strawberries

For dietary purposes, please note that this recipe contains alcohol. Alcohol can be replaced with 1 teaspoon orange extract.

1. Place chocolate and milk in a medium saucepan. Heat over medium heat until chocolate melts. Set aside.

2. Stir together egg substitute, SPLENDA® Granulated Sweetener, cornstarch and orange-flavored liqueur or brandy in a small mixing bowl. Add to chocolate mixture. Stir constantly. Cook over medium heat while stirring constantly, until mixture begins to thicken (approximately 3 to 4 minutes). Remove from heat and pour into the bowl of a blender or food processor. Blend or process briefly (10 to 20 seconds) to make a more creamy texture. Pour into medium bowl and cover.

3. Refrigerate chocolate mixture approximately 2 to 3 hours or until cool. Whip cream until stiff and fold into chocolate. Refrigerate overnight to set. Mousse will keep, refrigerated, for 3 days.

4. To serve, layer strawberries and mousse in 6 all-purpose wine glasses.

Makes 6 servings
¾ cup mousse, ½ cup strawberries

PREP TIME: 25 minutes

TOTAL TIME: 8 hours, 25 minutes

Nutrition Information per Serving:
Calories 210 (150 calories from fat), Total Fat 17 g, Saturated Fat 10 g, Protein 5 g, Carbohydrate 14 g, Cholesterol 30 mg, Fiber 4 g, Sodium 50 mg, Sugars 5 g

Easy Pumpkin Pie

¾ **cup SPLENDA® No Calorie Sweetener, Granulated**

2 **tablespoons light molasses**

¼ **teaspoon salt**

2 **teaspoons ground cinnamon**

4 **egg whites**

1 **(15-ounce) can pumpkin purée**

1¼ **cups nonfat evaporated milk**

1 **(9-inch) unbaked pie crust**

2 **cups fat-free frozen whipped topping, thawed**

1. Preheat oven to 350°F.

2. In a large mixing bowl, stir together SPLENDA® Granulated Sweetener, molasses, salt and cinnamon. Mix well. Stir in egg whites, pumpkin and milk. Pour into pie crust.

3. Bake in preheated oven 1¼ to 1½ hours or until a toothpick inserted into the pie comes out clean. Top with whipped topping before serving.

Makes 8 servings
1 slice (⅛ pie)

PREP TIME: 10 minutes

COOK TIME: 1 hour, 15 minutes

TOTAL TIME: 1 hour, 25 minutes

Nutrition Information per Serving:
Calories 220 (70 calories from fat), Total Fat 8 g, Saturated Fat 2 g, Protein 7 g, Carbohydrate 29 g, Cholesterol 0 mg, Fiber 3 g, Sodium 400 mg, Sugars 16 g

Frozen Mini Cinnamon Coffee Cheesecakes

12 **NABISCO® Ginger Snaps**

2 **tablespoons MAXWELL HOUSE® Naturally Decaffeinated Instant Coffee**

1 **tablespoon water**

½ **cup SPLENDA® No Calorie Sweetener, Granulated**

1 **(8-ounce) container PHILADELPHIA® Light Cream Cheese Spread**

1 **teaspoon vanilla extract**

¼ **teaspoon ground cinnamon**

1½ **cups thawed COOL WHIP® Whipped Topping**

1 **cup fresh raspberries**

1. Line 12 muffin tin cups with paper liners. Place 1 cookie in each paper cup. Set aside.

2. Mix coffee granules and water in large bowl until coffee is dissolved. Add SPLENDA® Granulated Sweetener, cream cheese spread, vanilla and cinnamon. Beat with wire whisk until well blended. Gently stir in whipped topping.

3. Spoon mixture evenly over cookies in muffin pan. Top each cheesecake with raspberries. Cover and freeze for 3 hours or overnight.

4. Remove from freezer about 10 minutes before serving to soften slightly.

Makes 12 servings
1 mini cheesecake

PREP TIME: 15 minutes

TOTAL TIME: 3 hours, 15 minutes

Nutrition Information per Serving:
Calories 35 (18 calories from fat), Total Fat 2 g, Saturated Fat 2 g, Protein 0 g, Carbohydrate 3 g, Cholesterol 0 mg, Fiber 1 g, Sodium 0 mg, Sugars 2 g

Fresh Strawberry Pie

⅓ **cup water**

1 **cup SPLENDA® No Calorie Sweetener, Granulated**

1 **(1-ounce) package unflavored gelatin**

⅓ **cup water**

6 **cups strawberries, cleaned and cut in half**

1 **(9-inch) prepared reduced-fat graham cracker crust**

1. Pour ⅓ cup water in a small mixing bowl. Add SPLENDA® Granulated Sweetener. Stir well. Sprinkle gelatin over the top. Let stand 1 minute.

2. Pour ⅓ cup water in a small pan. Boil. Pour boiling water over gelatin mixture. Stir until dissolved.

3. Refrigerate approximately 20 minutes or until the mixture begins to thicken. Stir frequently.

4. Toss with prepared berries and spoon into pie crust. Chill until set.

Makes 8 servings
1 slice (⅛ pie)

PREP TIME: 20 minutes

TOTAL TIME: 50 minutes

Nutrition Information per Serving:
Calories 140 (35 calories from fat), Total Fat 4 g, Saturated Fat 1 g, Protein 5 g, Carbohydrate 22 g, Cholesterol 0 mg, Fiber 3 g, Sodium 95 mg, Sugars 6 g

Beverages & Smoothies

Banana Punch Slush

- 4 **ripe bananas**
- ¾ **cup SPLENDA® No Calorie Sweetener, Granulated**
- 6 **cups water, divided**
- 1 **(46-fluid-ounce) can pineapple juice**
- 2 **(12-fluid-ounce) cans frozen orange juice concentrate**
- 1 **(12-fluid-ounce) can frozen lemonade concentrate**
- 3 **liters ginger ale**

1. In a blender, combine bananas, SPLENDA® Granulated Sweetener and 3 cups water. Blend until smooth. Pour into a large bowl and stir in pineapple juice. Stir in orange juice concentrate, lemonade concentrate and 3 more cups water. Divide into 3 plastic containers and freeze until solid.

2. Remove from freezer 3 to 4 hours before serving. Using 1 portion at a time, place slush in a punch bowl and pour in 1 liter of ginger ale for each.

Makes 54 servings
1 (4-fluid-ounce) drink

PREP TIME: 15 minutes

TOTAL TIME: 3 hours, 15 minutes

Nutrition Information per Serving:
Calories 80 (0 calories from fat), Total Fat 0 g, Saturated Fat 0 g, Protein 0 g, Carbohydrate 19 g, Cholesterol 0 mg, Fiber 0 g, Sodium 10 mg, Sugars 18 g

Caramel Latte

2 **sticks SPLENDA® Flavors for Coffee, Caramel**

¼ cup brewed espresso

¼ teaspoon vanilla extract

½ cup 2% reduced-fat milk

1. Mix all ingredients together in a microwaveable bowl or mug. Heat in microwave 30 to 40 seconds or to desired temperature.

2. Blend in blender 15 to 20 seconds to create a frothy drink, if desired. Pour into serving cup and serve immediately.

Makes 1 serving
1 (6-fluid-ounce) drink

PREP TIME: 5 minutes

TOTAL TIME: 5 minutes

Nutrition Information per Serving:
Calories 70 (20 calories from fat), Total Fat 2 g, Saturated Fat 2 g, Protein 4 g, Carbohydrate 9 g, Cholesterol 10 mg, Fiber 0 g, Sodium 70 mg, Sugars 6 g

Banana Strawberry Shake

1 **large ripe banana, sliced**

5 **packets SPLENDA® No Calorie Sweetener**

½ **cup 2% reduced-fat milk**

1¼ **cups frozen unsweetened strawberries**

Makes 2 servings
1 (8-fluid-ounce) drink

PREP TIME: 5 minutes

TOTAL TIME: 5 minutes

Nutrition Information per Serving:
Calories 140 (15 calories from fat), Total Fat 2 g, Saturated Fat 1 g, Protein 3 g, Carbohydrate 31 g, Cholesterol 5 mg, Fiber 5 g, Sodium 35 mg, Sugars 25 g

---

1. Combine all ingredients in a blender. Blend on medium speed until smooth.

2. Pour into glasses and serve.

KOOL-AID® *Fizzy Float*

- 1 **quart cold water**
- 2 **cups light white grape juice, chilled**
- 1 **cup SPLENDA® No Calorie Sweetener, Granulated**
- 1 **envelope of your favorite flavor KOOL-AID® Unsweetened Soft Drink Mix**
- 2 **cups seltzer water, chilled**
- 2 **cups no-sugar-added light vanilla ice cream**

1. Combine water, grape juice, SPLENDA® Granulated Sweetener and KOOL-AID® Soft Drink Mix in a pitcher, stirring until SPLENDA® Granulated Sweetener dissolves.

2. Pour ¾ cup of the mixture into each of 8 tall glasses; add ¼ cup of the seltzer to each glass. Top each serving with ¼ cup of the ice cream. Serve immediately. Store leftover prepared drink in refrigerator.

Makes 8 servings
1 (8-fluid-ounce) drink

PREP TIME: 10 minutes

TOTAL TIME: 10 minutes

Nutrition Information per Serving:
Calories 70 (20 calories from fat), Total Fat 2 g, Saturated Fat 1 g, Protein 1 g, Carbohydrate 15 g, Cholesterol 5 mg, Fiber 0 g, Sodium 40 mg, Sugars 7 g

Caramel Apple Cider

1 stick SPLENDA® No Calorie Sweetener Flavors for Coffee, Caramel

2 sticks SPLENDA® No Calorie Sweetener Flavors for Coffee, Cinnamon Spice

1 cup apple cider or apple juice

Mix all ingredients together in a large mug or coffee cup. Heat in microwave until warm. Serve immediately.

Makes 1 serving
1 (8-fluid-ounce) drink

PREP TIME: 5 minutes

TOTAL TIME: 5 minutes

Nutrition Information per Serving:
Calories 120 (0 calories from fat), Total Fat 0 g, Saturated Fat 0 g, Protein 0 g, Carbohydrate 32 g, Cholesterol 0 mg, Fiber 0 g, Sodium 25 mg, Sugars 26 g

Virgin Mojito

6 mint leaves

1 tablespoon SPLENDA® No Calorie Sweetener, Granulated

1 lime, juiced

1 (12-ounce) can diet lemon-lime soda, chilled

Fresh mint for garnish (optional)

Lime slices for garnish (optional)

1. Smash mint leaves and SPLENDA® Granulated Sweetener with a spoon in the bottom of a large glass.

2. Add lime juice and stir. Pour in soda and stir well.* Garnish with mint and lime slice, if desired. Serve chilled.

*A cocktail shaker can be used to create a frothier beverage. Add ice and mojito to a shaker and shake well.

Makes 1 serving
1 (12-fluid-ounce) drink

PREP TIME: 5 minutes

TOTAL TIME: 5 minutes

Nutrition Information per Serving:
Calories 20 (0 calories from fat), Total Fat 0 g, Saturated Fat 0 g, Protein 0 g, Carbohydrate 6 g, Cholesterol 0 mg, Fiber 0 g, Sodium 55 mg, Sugars 3 g

Mock Sangria

2 sticks SPLENDA® No Calorie Sweetener FLAVOR ACCENTS™, Lemon

1 thin slice fresh lemon

2 thin slices fresh orange

1 cup alcohol-removed wine

3 thin slices fresh apple

Ice, as desired

Makes 1 serving
1 (8-fluid-ounce) drink

PREP TIME: 5 minutes

TOTAL TIME: 5 minutes

Nutrition Information per Serving:
Calories 35 (0 calories from fat), Total Fat 0 g, Saturated Fat 0 g, Protein 1 g, Carbohydrate 10 g, Cholesterol 0 mg, Fiber 1 g, Sodium 25 mg, Sugars 7 g

Crush SPLENDA® No Calorie Sweetener FLAVOR ACCENTS™, lemon and orange slices with a fork in a tall glass. Add wine and stir. Add apple slices and ice, as desired. Serve immediately.

Berry Simple Smoothie

2 cups frozen unsweetened whole strawberries

1 cup fat-free plain yogurt

½ cup lite cranberry juice

¼ cup SPLENDA® No Calorie Sweetener, Granulated

Combine frozen strawberries, yogurt, cranberry juice and SPLENDA® Granulated Sweetener in a blender until smooth, stopping to scrape down sides.

Makes 3 servings
about 1 cup

PREP TIME: 5 minutes

TOTAL TIME: 5 minutes

Nutrition Information per Serving:
Calories 110 (0 calories from fat), Total Fat 0 g, Saturated Fat 0 g, Protein 5 g, Carbohydrate 22 g, Cholesterol 0 mg, Fiber 3 g, Sodium 65 mg, Sugars 18 g

Strawberry Orange Smash Smoothie

3 cups frozen strawberries, unsweetened

⅔ cup SPLENDA® No Calorie Sweetener, Granulated

1¼ cups orange juice, calcium fortified

1 cup plain nonfat yogurt

½ teaspoon vanilla extract

¼ cup ice cubes

Add all ingredients to blender. Blender will be full. Mix on low speed for 10 seconds. Remove lid, stir with wooden spoon.

Mix on medium speed 15 to 20 seconds; remove lid and stir again. Mix on high speed 15 to 20 seconds or until smooth. Pour into glasses. Serve immediately.

Makes 5 servings
1 (8-fluid-ounce) drink

PREP TIME: 10 minutes

TOTAL TIME: 10 minutes

Nutrition Information per Serving:
Calories 80 (0 calories from fat), Total Fat 0 g, Saturated Fat 0 g, Protein 3 g, Carbohydrate 19 g, Cholesterol 0 mg, Fiber 2 g, Sodium 30 mg, Sugars 14 g

Raspberry Hot Chocolate

2 sticks SPLENDA® No Calorie Sweetener FLAVOR ACCENTS™, Raspberry

1 packet sugar-free hot cocoa mix

1 cup 1% low-fat milk

1. Mix SPLENDA® No Calorie Sweetener FLAVOR ACCENTS™ and dry cocoa mix in a mug or coffee cup. Heat milk on stovetop or in microwave.

2. Pour hot milk into mug. Stir well. Serve immediately.

Makes 1 serving
1 (8-fluid-ounce) drink

PREP TIME: 2 minutes

TOTAL TIME: 2 minutes

Nutrition Information per Serving:
Calories 150 (25 calories from fat), Total Fat 3 g, Saturated Fat 2 g, Protein 12 g, Carbohydrate 22 g, Cholesterol 10 mg, Fiber 0 g, Sodium 220 mg, Sugars 19 g

Cookbook Index

After-School
    Butterscotch Brownies 54

Almond Cheesecake Bars 52

Apple Cranberry Pie 66

Apple Pie Oatmeal 6

Apricots and Ricotta
    Cheese Toast 8

Banana Mini-Chip Muffins 10

Banana Punch Slush 80

Banana Strawberry Shake 83

Bars & Brownies
    After-School Butterscotch
        Brownies 54

    Almond Cheesecake Bars 52

    Oat-Date Bars 56

Berry Simple Smoothie 89

Berry-Cherry Pie 70

Beverages & Smoothies
    Banana Punch Slush 80

    Banana Strawberry Shake 83

    Berry Simple Smoothie 89

    Caramel Apple Cider 86

    Caramel Latte 82

    KOOL-AID® Fizzy Float 84

    Mock Sangria 88

    Raspberry Hot Chocolate 92

    Strawberry Orange Smash
        Smoothie 90

    Virgin Mojito 87

Blueberry Corn Muffins 14

Boston-Style Baked Beans 29

Breakfast & Brunch Foods
Apple Pie Oatmeal 6

Apricots and Ricotta
    Cheese Toast 8

Banana Mini-Chip Muffins 10

Blueberry Corn Muffins 14

Cheery Cherry Muffins 16

Cinnamon-Pecan
    Monkey Bread 22

Crispy French Toast 20

Lemon-Orange
    Walnut Bread 18

Pistachio Cranberry
    Scones 12

Pumpkin Waffles 24

Caramel Apple Cider 86

Caramel Latte 82

Cheery Cherry Muffins 16

Chicken Cacciatore
    over Pasta 32

Chocolate Velvet Mousse 72

Cinnamon-Pecan
    Monkey Bread 22

Coconut-Date-Nut Balls 58

Cookies
Coconut-Date-Nut Balls 58

Merry Gingerbread Cookies . . 48

Old Fashioned Peanut
    Butter Chocolate
    Chip Cookies 46

Peanut Butter and
    Jelly Bites 60

Peanut Butter
    Cookie Bites 62

Sand Tarts 50

Tangy Coconut Tartlets 44

Crispy French Toast 20

Cookbook Index

Cucumber and
  Onion Salad 28

Desserts
Chocolate Velvet
  Mousse 72
Frozen Mini Cinnamon
  Coffee Cheesecakes 76

Easy Lemon Chicken 34

Easy Pumpkin Pie 74

Fluffy Carrot Soufflé 38

Fresh Strawberry Pie 78

Frozen Mini Cinnamon Coffee
  Cheesecakes 76

KOOL-AID® Fizzy Float 84

Lemon Glazed Jumbo
  Shrimp Salad 30

Lemon-Orange
  Walnut Bread 18

Main Dishes
Chicken Cacciatore
  over Pasta 32
Easy Lemon Chicken 34
Polynesian Pork Chops 36

Merry Gingerbread Cookies 48

Mock Sangria 88

Nostalgic Apple Pie 68

Oat-Date Bars 56

Old Fashioned Peanut
  Butter Chocolate
  Chip Cookies 46

Peanut Butter and Jelly Bites 60

Peanut Butter Cookie Bites 62

Pies
Apple Cranberry Pie 66
Berry-Cherry Pie 70
Easy Pumpkin Pie 74
Fresh Strawberry Pie 78
Nostalgic Apple Pie 68
S'mores Campfire Pie 64

Pistachio Cranberry Scones 12

Polynesian Pork Chops 36

Pumpkin Waffles 24

Raspberry Cocktail Sauce
  with Chilled Shrimp 26

Raspberry Hot Chocolate 92

Salads & Side Dishes
Boston-Style Baked Beans 29
Cucumber and Onion
  Salad 28
Fluffy Carrot Soufflé 38
Lemon Glazed Jumbo
  Shrimp Salad 30
Raspberry Cocktail Sauce
  with Chilled Shrimp 26
Sensational Pumpkin Bake . . . 42
Sweet Potato Casserole 40

Sand Tarts 50

Sensational Pumpkin Bake 42

S'mores Campfire Pie 64

Strawberry Orange
  Smash Smoothie 90

Sweet Potato Casserole 40

Tangy Coconut Tartlets 44

Virgin Mojito 87

Recipe Card Index

After-School Butterscotch
    Brownies 122

Almond Cheesecake Bars 122

Apple Cranberry Pie 128

Apple Pie Oatmeal 98

Apricots and Ricotta
    Cheese Toast . . . . , , . 98

Banana Mini-Chip Muffins. 100

Banana Punch Slush 136

Banana Strawberry Shake 138

Berry Simple Smoothie. 142

Berry-Cherry Pie 130

Blueberry Corn Muffins 102

Boston-Style Baked Beans. 110

Caramel Apple Cider 140

Caramel Latte 136

Cheery Cherry Muffins. 102

Chicken Cacciatore
    over Pasta. 112

Chocolate Velvet Mousse. 132

Cinnamon-Pecan
    Monkey Bread 106

Coconut-Date-Nut Balls 124

Crispy French Toast 104

Cucumber and
    Onion Salad 108

Easy Lemon Chicken. 112

Easy Pumpkin Pie 132

Fluffy Carrot Soufflé 114

Fresh Strawberry Pie. 134

Frozen Mini Cinnamon
    Coffee Cheesecakes 134

KOOL-AID® Fizzy Float 138

Lemon Glazed Jumbo
    Shrimp Salad. 110

Lemon-Orange
    Walnut Bread , ... 104

Merry Gingerbread Cookies. . . . 120

Mock Sangria 142

Nostalgic Apple Pie. 130

Out-Date Bars. 124

Old Fashioned Peanut
    Butter Chocolate
    Chip Cookies 118

Peanut Butter and Jelly Bites . . . 126

Peanut Butter Cookie Bites. 126

Pistachio Cranberry Scones 100

Polynesian Pork Chops 114

Pumpkin Waffles. 106

Raspberry Cocktail Sauce
    with Chilled Shrimp 108

Raspberry Hot Chocolate. 144

Sand Tarts 120

Sensational Pumpkin Bake 116

S'mores Campfire Pie 128

Strawberry Orange
    Smash Smoothie. 144

Sweet Potato Casserole 116

Tangy Coconut Tartlets 118

Virgin Mojito 140

Metric Chart

VOLUME MEASUREMENTS (dry)

1/8 teaspoon = 0.5 mL
1/4 teaspoon = 1 mL
1/2 teaspoon = 2 mL
3/4 teaspoon = 4 mL
1 teaspoon = 5 mL
1 tablespoon = 15 mL
2 tablespoons = 30 mL
1/4 cup = 60 mL
1/3 cup = 75 mL
1/2 cup = 125 mL
2/3 cup = 150 mL
3/4 cup = 175 mL
1 cup = 250 mL
2 cups = 1 pint = 500 mL
3 cups = 750 mL
4 cups = 1 quart = 1 L

VOLUME MEASUREMENTS (fluid)

1 fluid ounce (2 tablespoons) = 30 mL
4 fluid ounces (1/2 cup) = 125 mL
8 fluid ounces (1 cup) = 250 mL
12 fluid ounces (1 1/2 cups) = 375 mL
16 fluid ounces (2 cups) = 500 mL

WEIGHTS (mass)

1/2 ounce = 15 g
1 ounce = 30 g
3 ounces = 90 g
4 ounces = 120 g
8 ounces = 225 g
10 ounces = 285 g
12 ounces = 360 g
16 ounces = 1 pound = 450 g

DIMENSIONS

1/16 inch = 2 mm
1/8 inch = 3 mm
1/4 inch = 6 mm
1/2 inch = 1.5 cm
3/4 inch = 2 cm
1 inch = 2.5 cm

OVEN TEMPERATURES

250°F = 120°C
275°F = 140°C
300°F = 150°C
325°F = 160°C
350°F = 180°C
375°F = 190°C
400°F = 200°C
425°F = 220°C
450°F = 230°C

BAKING PAN SIZES

Utensil	Size in Inches/Quarts	Metric Volume	Size in Centimeters
Baking or Cake Pan (square or rectangular)	8×8×2	2 L	20×20×5
	9×9×2	2.5 L	23×23×5
	12×8×2	3 L	30×20×5
	13×9×2	3.5 L	33×23×5
Loaf Pan	8×4×3	1.5 L	20×10×7
	9×5×3	2 L	23×13×7
Round Layer Cake Pan	8×1½	1.2 L	20×4
	9×1½	1.5 L	23×4
Pie Plate	8×1¼	750 mL	20×3
	9×1¼	1 L	23×3
Baking Dish or Casserole	1 quart	1 L	—
	1½ quarts	1.5 L	—
	2 quarts	2 L	—

Apple Pie Oatmeal

Apricots and Ricotta Cheese Toast

Apple Pie Oatmeal

- **1 cup water**
- **½ cup old-fashioned oats**
- **1 dash salt (optional)**

Apple Pie Topping:

- **2 teaspoons SPLENDA® Brown Sugar Blend**
- **1 tablespoon chopped apple**
- **1 dash apple pie spice**

1. Stovetop Directions: Bring water to a boil in a small saucepan. Stir in oats and salt. Cook, stirring occasionally, over medium heat 5 minutes.

or

Microwave Directions: Combine water, oats and salt in a microwave-safe bowl. Cover tightly with heavy-duty plastic wrap; fold back a small edge to allow steam to escape. Microwave on high 2½ to 3 minutes; stir well.

2. Top oatmeal with SPLENDA® Brown Sugar Blend, chopped apple and spice.

Makes 1 serving
¾ cup oatmeal, 1 tablespoon sweetened chopped apple

PREP TIME: 10 minutes
TOTAL TIME: 10 minutes

Nutrition Information per Serving:
Calories 200 (25 calories from fat), Total Fat 3 g, Saturated Fat 0 g, Protein 7 g, Carbohydrate 37 g, Cholesterol 0 mg, Fiber 5 g, Sodium 400 mg, Sugars 10 g

Apricots and Ricotta Cheese Toast

- **1 cup water**
- **½ cup SPLENDA® Sugar Blend**
- **1 vanilla bean, split lengthwise**
- **1 lemon, zested**
- **6 fresh apricots, peeled, halved and pitted**
- **1 tablespoon butter, softened**
- **4 slices bread, toasted**
- **1 cup part-skim ricotta cheese**
  Optional Garnish: vanilla beans

1. Preheat broiler.

2. Combine water, SPLENDA® Sugar Blend, vanilla bean and lemon zest in a non-aluminum saucepan. Bring to a boil over medium heat, stirring until SPLENDA® Sugar Blend dissolves; reduce heat and simmer 10 minutes or until mixture is reduced. Add apricots and simmer for 3 to 5 minutes or until apricots are just tender. Using a slotted spoon, remove apricots from syrup. Set aside.

3. Spread butter on bread slices. Broil until bread is lightly toasted.

4. Spoon ricotta cheese on each bread slice. Top with apricots and remaining syrup. Broil 2 to 3 minutes or until thoroughly heated and apricots begin to caramelize. Garnish with a vanilla bean, if desired. Serve immediately.

Makes 4 servings
1 slice toast, ¼ cup ricotta, 3 apricot halves, 1 tablespoon syrup

PREP TIME: 10 minutes
COOK TIME: 18 minutes
TOTAL TIME: 28 minutes

Nutrition Information per Serving:
Calories 340 (80 calories from fat), Total Fat 9 g, Saturated Fat 5 g, Protein 10 g, Carbohydrate 49 g, Cholesterol 25 mg, Fiber 2 g, Sodium 240 mg, Sugars 34 g

Banana Mini-Chip Muffins

Pistachio Cranberry Scones

Banana Mini-Chip Muffins

- 2 **cups all-purpose flour**
- 2 **teaspoons baking powder**
- ½ **teaspoon salt**
- ¾ **cup light butter, softened**
- ⅓ **cup SPLENDA® Sugar Blend**
- ⅓ **cup packed SPLENDA® Brown Sugar Blend**
- 1 **teaspoon vanilla extract**
- 3 **medium ripe bananas, mashed**
- 1 **large egg**
- 1 **(12-ounce) package NESTLÉ® TOLL HOUSE® Semi-Sweet Chocolate Mini Morsels**

1. Preheat oven to 350°F. Spray 48 mini-muffin cups with nonstick cooking spray; set aside.

2. Combine flour, baking powder and salt in medium bowl; set aside.

3. Combine butter, SPLENDA® Sugar Blend, SPLENDA® Brown Sugar Blend and vanilla in large bowl; beat at medium speed with a mixer until creamy. Beat in bananas and egg. Gradually mix in flour mixture; stir in morsels. Spoon batter evenly into prepared pan, filling cups two-thirds full.

4. Bake 15 to 20 minutes or until a toothpick inserted in the centers comes out clean. Cool 10 minutes in pans on wire rack. Remove muffins from pans to wire rack to cool completely.

Makes 48 servings
1 mini-muffin

PREP TIME: 10 minutes
COOK TIME: 20 minutes
TOTAL TIME: 40 minutes

Nutrition Information per Serving:
Calories 90 (35 calories from fat), Total Fat 4 g, Saturated Fat 2 g, Protein 1 g, Carbohydrate 13 g, Cholesterol 10 mg, Fiber 0 g, Sodium 55 mg, Sugars 8 g

Pistachio Cranberry Scones

- 3 **cups all-purpose flour**
- 1½ **teaspoons cream of tartar**
- ¾ **teaspoon baking soda**
- ½ **teaspoon salt**
- 1 **tablespoon orange zest**
- 6 **tablespoons butter**
- ⅓ **cup SPLENDA® No Calorie Sweetener, Granulated**
- ¾ **cup 1% low-fat milk**
- ½ **cup dried cranberries**
- ½ **cup chopped pistachio nuts**

1. Preheat oven to 425°F. Spray a cookie sheet with nonstick cooking spray.

2. Combine flour, cream of tartar, baking soda, salt and orange zest in a large bowl; cut in butter with a pastry blender until mixture is crumbly. Add SPLENDA® Granulated Sweetener and milk to dry ingredients, stirring just until dry ingredients are moistened. Stir in cranberries and pistachio nuts.

3. Pat dough to a ¾-inch thickness on a lightly floured surface. Cut scones with a 2½-inch round biscuit cutter and place on cookie sheet.

4. Bake in preheated oven 12 to 15 minutes or until lightly browned.

Makes 14 servings
1 scone

PREP TIME: 10 minutes
COOK TIME: 15 minutes
TOTAL TIME: 25 minutes

Nutrition Information per Serving:
Calories 190 (70 calories from fat), Total Fat 7 g, Saturated Fat 3 g, Protein 4 g, Carbohydrate 26 g, Cholesterol 15 mg, Fiber 2 g, Sodium 230 mg, Sugars 4 g

Blueberry Corn Muffins

Cheery Cherry Muffins

Blueberry Corn Muffins

- 1¾ **cups all-purpose flour**
- ½ **cup yellow cornmeal**
- 1¼ **teaspoons baking powder**
- ½ **teaspoon baking soda**
- ½ **teaspoon salt**
- ¾ **cup SPLENDA® No Calorie Sweetener, Granulated**
- ½ **cup unsalted butter, softened**
- ⅓ **cup egg substitute**
- 2 **teaspoons vanilla**
- 1 **cup buttermilk**
- 1 **cup blueberries (frozen or fresh)**

1. Preheat oven to 350°F. Spray a muffin pan with nonstick cooking spray or line muffin cups with paper liners. Set aside.

2. Blend dry ingredients together in a medium mixing bowl. Set aside.

3. Blend butter in a large mixing bowl until light and fluffy. Add egg substitute slowly. Scrape sides and continue to mix until butter forms small lumps. Add vanilla and buttermilk. Mix well. Add dry ingredients in 3 batches. Mix well and scrape the sides of the bowl after each addition.

4. Fold blueberries gently into batter. Scoop batter into prepared muffin cups, filling cups to the top. Bake in preheated oven 20 to 25 minutes or until done.

Makes 10 servings
1 muffin

PREP TIME: 10 minutes
COOK TIME: 25 minutes
TOTAL TIME: 35 minutes

Nutrition Information per Serving:
Calories 210 (90 calories from fat), Total Fat 10 g, Saturated Fat 6 g, Protein 5 g, Carbohydrate 26 g, Cholesterol 25 mg, Fiber 1 g, Sodium 280 mg, Sugars 2 g

Cheery Cherry Muffins

- ½ **pound fresh or frozen cherries, pitted**
- ¼ **cup margarine**
- ¼ **cup reduced-fat cream cheese**
- ½ **cup SPLENDA® No Calorie Sweetener, Granulated**
- 1 **large egg**
- 2 **cups self-rising flour, sifted**
- 1 **cup nonfat milk**

1. Preheat oven to 400°F. Line a 12-cup muffin tin with paper liners. Lightly spray liners with nonstick cooking spray.

2. Set aside 12 cherries. Chop remaining cherries. Place cherries on a paper towel to drain.

3. Beat margarine and cream cheese at medium speed with an electric mixer until creamy. Add SPLENDA® Granulated Sweetener, beating well. Add egg, beating until blended.

4. Add flour to margarine mixture alternately with milk, beginning and ending with flour. Beat at low speed until blended after each addition. Do not overbeat. Stir in chopped cherries. Spoon 1 tablespoon of batter into each muffin cup. Place a cherry in the center of each cup. Top with remaining batter, filling muffin cups three-fourths full.

5. Bake in preheated oven 25 minutes or until muffins are lightly browned. Remove from pans immediately and cool on wire racks.

Makes 12 servings
1 muffin

PREP TIME: 20 minutes
COOK TIME: 25 minutes
TOTAL TIME: 45 minutes

Nutrition Information per Serving:
Calories 150 (50 calories from fat), Total Fat 6 g, Saturated Fat 1 g, Protein 4 g, Carbohydrate 21 g, Cholesterol 20 mg, Fiber 1 g, Sodium 340 mg, Sugars 5 g

Lemon-Orange Walnut Bread

Crispy French Toast

Lemon-Orange Walnut Bread

- 2 cups all-purpose flour
- 1 teaspoon baking powder
- ½ teaspoon baking soda
- ⅔ cup 1% low-fat milk
- 2 tablespoons lemon juice
- 1½ teaspoons freshly grated lemon peel
- 1½ teaspoons freshly grated orange peel
- 2 large eggs
- ¾ cup SPLENDA® No Calorie Sweetener, Granulated
- ½ cup butter, melted
- 2 teaspoons vanilla extract
- ¾ cup chopped walnuts

1. Preheat oven to 350°F. Lightly spray an 8½×4½×2½-inch loaf pan with nonstick cooking spray.

2. Combine flour, baking powder and baking soda. Set aside.

3. Combine milk, lemon juice, lemon and orange peels. Set aside.

4. Beat eggs and SPLENDA® Granulated Sweetener on high speed with an electric mixer 5 minutes. Reduce speed to medium; gradually add melted butter and vanilla, beating until blended, about 1 minute.

5. Add flour mixture alternately with milk mixture; beginning and ending with flour mixture.

Beat at low speed until blended after each addition. Stir in walnuts. Spoon batter into prepared loaf pan.

6. Bake in preheated oven 30 to 35 minutes or until a long wooden pick inserted in center comes out clean. Cool in pan on a wire rack 10 minutes; remove from pan and cool completely.

Makes 12 servings
1 (½-inch) slice

PREP TIME: 20 minutes
COOK TIME: 35 minutes
TOTAL TIME: 55 minutes

Nutrition Information per Serving:
Calories 220 (120 calories from fat), Total Fat 14 g, Saturated Fat 6 g, Protein 5 g, Carbohydrate 20 g, Cholesterol 55 mg, Fiber 1 g, Sodium 190 mg, Sugars 3 g

Crispy French Toast

- 1 cup 1% low-fat milk
- ¾ cup half and half
- ½ cup SPLENDA® No Calorie Sweetener, Granulated
- 2 tablespoons vanilla extract
- 4 large eggs
- 6 thick slices white bread, crusts removed and cut diagonally in half
- 4 cups cornflakes cereal, finely crushed
- 2 tablespoons ground cinnamon
- 1 cup strawberries, sliced
- 1 cup fat-free vanilla yogurt

Optional Garnish: fresh mint sprigs

1. Preheat oven to 350°F.

2. Combine milk, half and half, SPLENDA® Granulated Sweetener and vanilla; whisk until SPLENDA® Granulated Sweetener dissolves. Add eggs, whisking until blended.

3. Dip bread into the milk mixture; dredge in cornflakes cereal. Place on a baking sheet.

4. Bake in preheated oven 5 to 10 minutes or until golden brown.

5. Sprinkle a small amount of cinnamon over 6 plates. Arrange 2 toast triangles in the center of each plate. Arrange strawberries around toast; top toast with a small scoop of vanilla yogurt. Sprinkle with cinnamon. Garnish with fresh mint sprigs, if desired.

Makes 6 servings
1 slice French toast, 3 tablespoons strawberries, 3 tablespoons yogurt

PREP TIME: 10 minutes
COOK TIME: 10 minutes
TOTAL TIME: 20 minutes

Nutrition Information per Serving:
Calories 320 (80 calories from fat), Total Fat 9 g, Saturated Fat 4 g, Protein 12 g, Carbohydrate 44 g, Cholesterol 155 mg, Fiber 3 g, Sodium 460 mg, Sugars 10 g

Cinnamon-Pecan Monkey Bread

Pumpkin Waffles

Cinnamon-Pecan Monkey Bread

- ¼ **cup chopped pecans**
- 2 **tablespoons butter**
- ¼ **cup SPLENDA® Brown Sugar Blend**
- ¼ **teaspoon ground cinnamon**
- ⅓ **cup SPLENDA® Brown Sugar Blend**
- ¼ **teaspoon ground cinnamon**
- ½ **(3-pound) package frozen roll dough, thawed**
- 3 **tablespoons butter, melted**

1. Spray a 12-cup bundt pan with nonstick cooking spray. Sprinkle pecans in bottom of pan; set aside.

2. Combine 2 tablespoons butter, ¼ cup SPLENDA® Brown Sugar Blend and ¼ teaspoon cinnamon in a small saucepan; cook over low heat, stirring constantly until blended; pour mixture over pecans. Set aside.

3. Combine ⅓ cup SPLENDA® Brown Sugar Blend and ¼ teaspoon cinnamon in a small bowl; set aside.

4. Cut each roll into half; dip tops of balls into melted butter and then into SPLENDA® Brown Sugar Blend mixture. Place in prepared pan. (At this point Monkey Bread may be covered and stored in the refrigerator 8 hours or overnight, or proceed as directed). Cover and let rise in a warm place, free from drafts, 50 minutes or until doubled in bulk.

5. Preheat oven to 350°F about 10 minutes prior to baking. Bake 25 to 30 minutes or until bread sounds hollow when tapped. Remove from pan; cool on a wire rack. Serve warm.

Makes 18 servings
1 slice (1/18 of monkey bread)

PREP TIME: 20 minutes
COOK TIME: 25 minutes
TOTAL TIME: 1 hour, 35 minutes

Nutrition Information per Serving:
Calories 180 (60 calories from fat), Total Fat 6 g, Saturated Fat 2 g, Protein 4 g, Carbohydrate 24 g, Cholesterol 10 mg, Fiber 1 g, Sodium 290 mg, Sugars 9 g

Pumpkin Waffles

- 1 **cup all-purpose flour**
- 1 **teaspoon baking powder**
- ½ **teaspoon baking soda**
- ¼ **teaspoon salt**
- ¾ **teaspoon ground cinnamon**
- ½ **teaspoon ground ginger**
- ⅛ **teaspoon ground nutmeg**
- 2 **teaspoons canola oil**
- 1 **teaspoon molasses**
- ¼ **cup canned pumpkin**
- 1 **cup buttermilk**
- 1 **large egg**
- 2 **tablespoons SPLENDA® No Calorie Sweetener, Granulated**
- 1½ **cups maple syrup sweetened with SPLENDA® Brand Sweetener**

1. Preheat waffle iron according to manufacturer's directions; spray lightly with nonstick cooking spray.

2. Combine flour, baking powder, baking soda, salt, cinnamon, ginger and nutmeg in a large bowl. Set aside.

3. Combine oil, molasses, pumpkin and buttermilk in a small bowl. Set aside.

4. Whisk together egg and SPLENDA® Granulated Sweetener until blended. Add buttermilk mixture, whisking until blended. Add to dry ingredients, stirring just until moistened.

5. Pour batter into hot waffle iron and bake approximately 5 minutes. Serve with maple syrup.

Makes 6 servings
1 waffle

PREP TIME: 15 minutes
COOK TIME: 5 minutes
TOTAL TIME: 20 minutes

Nutrition Information per Serving:
Calories 160 (25 calories from fat), Total Fat 3 g, Saturated Fat 1 g, Protein 5 g, Carbohydrate 32 g, Cholesterol 35 mg, Fiber 1 g, Sodium 400 mg, Sugars 3 g

Raspberry Cocktail Sauce
with Chilled Shrimp

Cucumber and Onion Salad

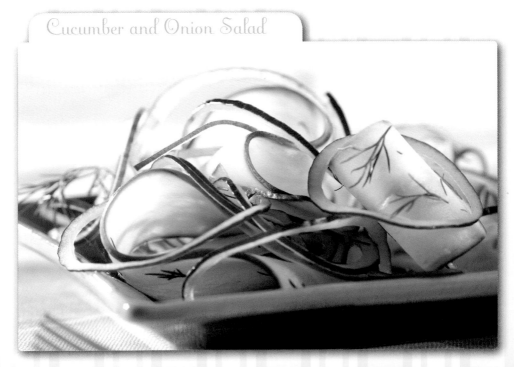

Raspberry Cocktail Sauce with Chilled Shrimp

Cocktail Sauce:

- 1 **cup no-sugar-added raspberry preserves**
- ¼ **cup prepared horseradish**
- 3 **tablespoons SPLENDA® No Calorie Sweetener, Granulated**
- 2 **tablespoons tomato paste**
- 3 **teaspoons sherry wine vinegar**
- 2 **tablespoons Worcestershire sauce**
- 1 **clove garlic, minced**

- 1 **jalapeño pepper, minced**
- ½ **teaspoon salt**
- 1 **pinch black pepper**

- 2 **pounds cooked, peeled and deveined shrimp**

1. Place cocktail sauce ingredients in a food processor or a blender. Process or blend for 30 seconds or until smooth.

2. Chill cocktail sauce at least 2 hours before serving. Serve with shrimp. Cocktail sauce will keep, refrigerated, for 5 days.

Makes 32 servings
2 shrimp, 1 tablespoon sauce

PREP TIME: 5 minutes
TOTAL TIME: 2 hours, 5 minutes

Nutrition Information per Serving:
Calories 45 (0 calories from fat),
Total Fat 0 g, Saturated Fat 0 g,
Protein 6 g, Carbohydrate 4 g,
Cholesterol 55 mg, Fiber 1 g,
Sodium 125 mg, Sugars 3 g

Cucumber and Onion Salad

- 2½ **cups thinly sliced unpeeled cucumbers**
- ½ **cup thinly sliced red onions**
- ⅓ **cup SPLENDA® No Calorie Sweetener, Granulated**
- ⅓ **cup white vinegar**
- ¼ **teaspoon salt**
- ⅛ **teaspoon black pepper**

1. Place cucumbers and onions in a non-metallic medium bowl.

2. Combine remaining ingredients in a small mixing bowl. Stir well. Pour over cucumbers and onions. Cover and refrigerate for at least 2 hours. Stir occasionally.

Makes 6 servings
¾ cup salad

PREP TIME: 15 minutes
TOTAL TIME: 2 hours, 15 minutes

Nutrition Information per Serving:
Calories 15 (0 calories from fat),
Total Fat 0 g, Saturated Fat 0 g,
Protein 1 g, Carbohydrate 3 g,
Cholesterol 0 mg, Fiber 1 g,
Sodium 100 mg, Sugars 2 g

Boston-Style Baked Beans

Lemon Glazed Jumbo Shrimp Salad

Boston-Style Baked Beans

- **4** **(15-ounce) cans navy beans**
- **½** **pound bacon, chopped**
- **1** **medium onion, chopped**
- **¼** **cup yellow mustard**
- **⅓** **cup SPLENDA® No Calorie Sweetener, Granulated**
- **2** **tablespoons robust molasses**

1. Preheat oven to 350°F.

2. Drain navy beans and reserve 1¼ cups liquid.

3. Cook bacon in a large skillet until browned. Remove bacon and reserve half of the bacon fat.

4. Cook onion in reserved bacon fat and cook until translucent. Stir in beans and remaining ingredients.

5. Pour beans into a 3-quart baking dish. Bake in preheated oven 45 minutes.

Makes 18 servings
½ cup

PREP TIME: 15 minutes
COOK TIME: 45 minutes
TOTAL TIME: 1 hour

Nutrition Information per Serving:
Calories 140 (25 calories from fat), Total Fat 3 g, Saturated Fat 1 g, Protein 9 g, Carbohydrate 21 g, Cholesterol 5 mg, Fiber 5 g, Sodium 520 mg, Sugars 3 g

Lemon Glazed Jumbo Shrimp Salad

- **1** **tablespoon extra-virgin olive oil**
- **8** **jumbo shrimp, peeled and deveined**
- **½** **cup fresh lemon juice**
- **½** **cup cider vinegar**
- **½** **cup SPLENDA® No Calorie Sweetener, Granulated**
- **½** **teaspoon crushed red pepper**
- **1** **jalapeño, trimmed, seeded and thinly sliced**
- **2** **cups baby arugula leaves**
- **½** **cup thinly sliced red bell pepper**
- **½** **cup thinly sliced mango**
- **Salt and pepper to taste**

1. Heat oil in a medium skillet over high heat; add shrimp and cook 1 minute. Stir in lemon juice and cook 3 to 4 minutes or until shrimp are cooked through. Using tongs, transfer shrimp to a plate. Add vinegar, SPLENDA® Granulated Sweetener, crushed red pepper and jalapeño; bring to a boil and cook 4 to 5 minutes or until reduced by half, then remove from heat and set aside.

2. Place arugula, red pepper and mango in a large bowl; toss gently with some of the dressing and season to taste.

3. Divide arugula mixture among 4 serving plates; top each salad with 2 shrimp and drizzle evenly with the warm vinegar mixture.

Makes 4 servings
2 jumbo shrimp, ¾ cup salad

PREP TIME: 10 minutes
COOK TIME: 12 minutes
TOTAL TIME: 22 minutes

Nutrition Information per Serving:
Calories 120 (40 calories from fat), Total Fat 4 g, Saturated Fat 1 g, Protein 12 g, Carbohydrate 10 g, Cholesterol 105 mg, Fiber 1 g, Sodium 220 mg, Sugars 6 g

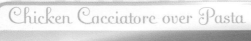

Chicken Cacciatore over Pasta

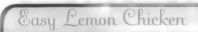

Easy Lemon Chicken

Chicken Cacciatore over Pasta

- 1 **pound boneless, skinless chicken breast halves**
- ½ **cup chopped onion**
- ½ **cup chopped green bell pepper**
- 1 **(16-ounce) can chopped tomatoes, drained**
- 1 **(8-ounce) can tomato sauce**
- 2 **tablespoons SPLENDA® No Calorie Sweetener, Granulated**
- 1½ **teaspoons Italian seasoning**
- ⅓ **cup sliced ripe olives**
- ⅛ **teaspoon black pepper**

- 3 **cups hot cooked noodles (or any favorite pasta), rinsed and drained**

1. Slice chicken breasts into 32 pieces.

2. Spray a large skillet with olive oil-flavored nonstick cooking spray. Sauté chicken, onion and green pepper for 6 to 8 minutes. Stir in drained tomatoes and tomato sauce.

3. Add SPLENDA® Granulated Sweetener, Italian seasoning, olives and black pepper. Mix well to combine. Lower heat and simmer for 10 to 15 minutes, stirring occasionally.

4. For each serving, place ½ cup pasta on a plate and spoon ⅔ cup chicken and sauce mixture over top.

Makes 6 servings
½ cup noodles, ¾ cup chicken cacciatore

PREP TIME: 10 minutes
COOK TIME: 23 minutes
TOTAL TIME: 33 minutes

Nutrition Information per Serving:
Calories 210 (40 calories from fat), Total Fat 4 g, Saturated Fat 1 g, Protein 21 g, Carbohydrate 22 g, Cholesterol 65 mg, Fiber 3 g, Sodium 460 mg, Sugars 5 g

Easy Lemon Chicken

- 1 **teaspoon cornstarch**
- 1 **tablespoon low-sodium soy sauce**
- 12 **ounces chicken breast tenders, cut into thirds**
- ¼ **cup fresh lemon juice**
- ¼ **cup low-sodium soy sauce**
- ¼ **cup fat-free chicken broth**
- 1 **teaspoon fresh ginger, minced**
- 2 **cloves garlic, minced**
- 1 **tablespoon SPLENDA® No Calorie Sweetener, Granulated**
- 1 **teaspoon cornstarch**
- 1 **tablespoon vegetable oil**

- ¼ **cup red bell pepper, sliced into 2-inch strips**
- ¼ **cup green bell pepper, sliced into 2-inch strips**

1. Mix 1 teaspoon cornstarch and 1 tablespoon soy sauce in a small mixing bowl. Add sliced chicken tenders. Place in refrigerator and marinate for 10 minutes.

2. Stir the lemon juice, ¼ cup soy sauce, chicken broth, ginger, garlic, SPLENDA® Granulated Sweetener and 1 teaspoon cornstarch together in a medium mixing bowl.

3. Heat oil in a medium skillet. Add chicken and cook over medium-high heat 3 to 4 minutes or until just done. Add sauce and sliced peppers. Cook 1 to 2 minutes more or until sauce thickens and peppers are slightly tender.

Makes 4 servings
¾ cup lemon chicken

PREP TIME: 10 minutes
COOK TIME: 10 minutes
TOTAL TIME: 20 minutes

Nutrition Information per Serving:
Calories 150 (40 calories from fat), Total Fat 5 g, Saturated Fat 1 g, Protein 21 g, Carbohydrate 6 g, Cholesterol 50 mg, Fiber 1 g, Sodium 730 mg, Sugars 1 g

Polynesian Pork Chops

Fluffy Carrot Soufflé

Polynesian Pork Chops

- ½ **cup vegetable oil**
- 6 **lean pork chops**
- 2 **large eggs**
- 1 **cup all-purpose flour**
- 1 **(29-ounce) can diced peaches with heavy syrup**
- ½ **cup SPLENDA® Brown Sugar Blend**
- ½ **cup water, or as needed**

1. Heat oil in a skillet over medium heat.

2. Clean and de-bone the pork chops. In a small bowl, whisk eggs and set aside. In another bowl, add flour and any additional spices, if desired. Dip pork chops in egg and then flour.

3. Place the coated pork chops into the skillet.

4. Cook for 25 minutes, turning as needed.

5. Turn the heat to low; add peaches and SPLENDA® Brown Sugar Blend to the skillet on top of the pork chops. Add water if the chops look too dry.

6. Simmer for 10 minutes and serve.

Makes 6 servings
1 pork chop, ½ cup diced peach sauce

PREP TIME: 2 minutes
COOK TIME: 35 minutes
TOTAL TIME: 37 minutes

Nutrition Information per Serving:
Calories 590 (240 calories from fat), Total Fat 27 g, Saturated Fat 6 g, Protein 34 g, Carbohydrate 48 g, Cholesterol 145 mg, Fiber 2 g, Sodium 85 mg, Sugars 30 g

Fluffy Carrot Soufflé

- 1 **pound baby carrots**
- 2 **cups water**
- ½ **teaspoon salt**
- ¼ **cup butter**
- 3 **tablespoons all-purpose flour**
- 1 **teaspoon baking powder**
- ¼ **cup SPLENDA® No Calorie Sweetener, Granulated**
- 3 **large eggs**
- 1 **teaspoon vanilla extract**

1. Preheat oven to 350°F.

2. Combine carrots, water and salt in a medium saucepan; bring to a boil. Reduce heat and cook, covered, 12 to 15 minutes or until carrots are tender. Drain.

3. Process carrots and butter in a food processor until smooth, stopping once to scrape down sides.

4. Combine flour, baking powder and SPLENDA® Granulated Sweetener, add to carrot mixture and process until blended. Add eggs, one at a time, and process until blended. Add vanilla and pulse 2 or 3 times.

5. Spoon mixture into a greased 1-quart baking dish.

6. Bake in preheated oven 30 to 45 minutes or until thoroughly heated.

7. Serve immediately.

Makes 5 servings
½ cup soufflé

PREP TIME: 30 minutes
COOK TIME: 45 minutes
TOTAL TIME: 1 hour, 15 minutes

Nutrition Information per Serving:
Calories 180 (120 calories from fat), Total Fat 13 g, Saturated Fat 7 g, Protein 5 g, Carbohydrate 13 g, Cholesterol 150 mg, Fiber 2 g, Sodium 450 mg, Sugars 6 g

Sweet Potato Casserole

Sensational Pumpkin Bake

Sweet Potato Casserole

- **4 medium sweet potatoes**
- **¾ cup SPLENDA® No Calorie Sweetener, Granulated**
- **½ cup whole milk**
- **2 teaspoons grated orange zest**
- **¼ cup fresh orange juice**
- **2 teaspoons vanilla extract**
- **1 large egg, lightly beaten**
- **½ cup all-purpose flour**
- **3 tablespoons butter, melted**
- **1 cup panko bread crumbs**
- **½ cup finely chopped pecans**
- **2 tablespoons butter, melted**
- **3 tablespoons maple syrup**

1. Preheat oven to 375°F. Lightly grease a 13×9-inch baking dish.

2. Place sweet potatoes on a baking sheet; bake in preheated oven 1 hour or until done. Cool to touch. Peel and mash. Reduce oven to 350°F.

3. Combine sweet potatoes and next 8 ingredients in a large bowl. Beat at medium speed with an electric mixer until smooth. Spoon into baking dish.

4. Combine panko and remaining ingredients; sprinkle crumb mixture over top of casserole. Bake an additional 1 hour or until casserole is thoroughly heated.

Makes 14 servings
½ cup sweet potato casserole

PREP TIME: 10 minutes
COOK TIME: 2 hours
TOTAL TIME: 2 hours, 10 minutes

Nutrition Information per Serving:
Calories 190 (70 calories from fat), Total Fat 8 g, Saturated Fat 3 g, Protein 4 g, Carbohydrate 29 g, Cholesterol 30 mg, Fiber 3 g, Sodium 95 mg, Sugars 10 g

Sensational Pumpkin Bake

- **2 (15-ounce) cans 100% pure pumpkin**
- **4 tablespoons SPLENDA® Brown Sugar Blend, divided**
- **¼ cup butter or margarine**
- **¼ teaspoon ground cinnamon**
- **⅛ teaspoon ground nutmeg**
- **¼ cup chopped pecans, toasted**

1. Preheat oven to 350°F.

2. Combine pumpkin, 3 tablespoons of the SPLENDA® Brown Sugar Blend, butter, cinnamon and nutmeg in medium saucepan. Cook over medium heat, stirring occasionally, until mixture comes to a boil. Reduce heat to low; cook 1 to 2 minutes. Pour hot mixture into an ungreased 1½-quart casserole dish. Combine remaining 1 tablespoon of the SPLENDA® Brown Sugar Blend and pecans in small bowl. Sprinkle over pumpkin.

3. Bake in preheated oven 5 to 10 minutes or until browned.

Makes 8 servings
½ cup pumpkin bake

PREP TIME: 15 minutes
COOK TIME: 10 minutes
TOTAL TIME: 25 minutes

Nutrition Information per Serving:
Calories 150 (80 calories from fat), Total Fat 9 g, Saturated Fat 4 g, Protein 2 g, Carbohydrate 17 g, Cholesterol 15 mg, Fiber 3 g, Sodium 320 mg, Sugars 11 g

Tangy Coconut Tartlets

Old Fashioned Peanut Butter Chocolate Chip Cookies

Tangy Coconut Tartlets

1½ **cups sweetened flaked coconut**

¼ **cup SPLENDA® No Calorie Sweetener, Granulated**

¾ **cup all-purpose flour**

2 **teaspoons vanilla extract**

2 **egg whites**

1 **(3.4-ounce) package instant lemon pudding mix**

2 **cups nonfat milk**

1 **(8-ounce) container fat-free frozen whipped topping, thawed**

1 **tablespoon unsweetened flaked coconut, toasted**

1. Preheat oven to 400°F. Lightly grease 24 mini-muffin cups.

2. In a mixing bowl, combine 1½ cups coconut, SPLENDA® Granulated Sweetener, flour, vanilla and egg whites; stir well. Divide mixture evenly among the prepared mini-muffin cups, pressing mixture into bottom and up sides of muffin cups.

3. Bake in preheated oven until the edges are browned. Cool 2 minutes in the muffin tins on a wire rack. Remove from tins and cool completely on a wire rack.

4. Prepare lemon pudding according to package instructions using the milk. Spoon lemon mixture into each macaroon tartlet shell. Top with 2 teaspoons of whipped topping sprinkled with a pinch of toasted coconut.

Makes 24 servings
1 tartlet

PREP TIME: 20 minutes
COOK TIME: 20 minutes
TOTAL TIME: 40 minutes

Nutrition Information per Serving:
Calories 80 (15 calories from fat), Total Fat 2 g, Saturated Fat 1 g, Protein 2 g, Carbohydrate 13 g, Cholesterol 0 mg, Fiber 0 g, Sodium 85 mg, Sugars 7 g

Old Fashioned Peanut Butter Chocolate Chip Cookies

1½ **cups all-purpose flour**

1 **teaspoon baking soda**

1 **cup butter or margarine, softened**

½ **cup creamy or chunky peanut butter**

½ **cup SPLENDA® Sugar Blend**

½ **cup SPLENDA® Brown Sugar Blend, packed**

1 **teaspoon vanilla extract**

1 **large egg**

1⅓ **cups NESTLÉ® TOLL HOUSE® Peanut Butter & Milk Chocolate Morsels**

1. Preheat oven to 375°F.

2. Combine flour and baking soda in small bowl. Set aside.

3. Beat butter, peanut butter, SPLENDA® Sugar Blend, SPLENDA® Brown Sugar Blend and vanilla in large bowl until creamy. Beat in egg. Gradually beat in flour mixture. Stir in morsels.

4. Drop dough by rounded tablespoons onto ungreased baking sheets. Press down slightly with bottom of glass dipped in SPLENDA® Sugar Blend.

5. Bake in preheated oven 8 to 10 minutes or until edges are set but centers are still soft. Cool on baking sheets 4 minutes. Remove to wire racks to cool completely.

Makes 36 servings
1 cookie

PREP TIME: 10 minutes
COOK TIME: 10 minutes
TOTAL TIME: 20 minutes

Nutrition Information per Serving:
Calories 120 (70 calories from fat), Total Fat 7 g, Saturated Fat 4 g, Protein 2 g, Carbohydrate 11 g, Cholesterol 20 mg, Fiber 0 g, Sodium 105 mg, Sugars 7 g

Merry Gingerbread Cookies

Sand Tarts

Merry Gingerbread Cookies

- 6 **cups all-purpose flour**
- 1 **teaspoon baking soda**
- ½ **teaspoon baking powder**
- 4 **teaspoons ground ginger**
- 4 **teaspoons ground cinnamon**
- 1½ **teaspoons ground cloves**
- 1 **cup unsalted butter, softened**
- 1 **cup SPLENDA® No Calorie Sweetener, Granulated**
- 1 **teaspoon salt**
- 2 **large eggs**
- 1 **cup molasses**
- 3 **tablespoons water**

1. Blend together flour, baking soda, baking powder and spices in a large mixing bowl.

2. Cream butter, SPLENDA® Granulated Sweetener and salt together in a large mixing bowl. Add eggs, one at a time, beating well after each addition. Add molasses and water. Stir well. Add flour mixture and stir until well blended. Refrigerate dough 1 to 2 hours before rolling out and cutting into shapes.

3. Preheat oven to 350°F. Roll cookie dough out slightly less than ¼-inch thick. Cut into desired shapes. Bake in preheated oven 8 to 10 minutes or until lightly browned on the bottom.

Makes 54 servings
1 cookie

PREP TIME: 30 minutes
COOK TIME: 10 minutes
TOTAL TIME: 1 hour, 40 minutes

Nutrition Information per Serving:
Calories 100 (35 calories from fat), Total Fat 4 g, Saturated Fat 2 g, Protein 2 g, Carbohydrate 15 g, Cholesterol 15 mg, Fiber 1 g, Sodium 75 mg, Sugars 4 g

Sand Tarts

- 1 **cup butter, softened**
- ¼ **cup SPLENDA® No Calorie Sweetener, Granulated**
- 2 **cups all-purpose flour**
- 2 **teaspoons vanilla extract**
- 1 **cup chopped pecans**
- 2 **tablespoons SPLENDA® No Calorie Sweetener, Granulated**
- 2 **teaspoons cornstarch**

1. Preheat oven to 350°F.

2. Beat butter and ¼ cup SPLENDA® Granulated Sweetener at medium speed with an electric mixer about 2 minutes or until creamy. Gradually add flour, beating at low speed until blended. Stir in vanilla and pecans. Shape into 1-inch balls.

3. Bake in preheated oven 20 minutes; remove from oven and place on wire racks to cool.

4. Process 2 tablespoons SPLENDA® Granulated Sweetener and cornstarch in a blender or food processor; roll cookies in powdered SPLENDA® Granulated Sweetener mixture.

Makes 42 servings
1 cookie

PREP TIME: 15 minutes
COOK TIME: 20 minutes
TOTAL TIME: 35 minutes

Nutrition Information per Serving:
Calories 80 (60 calories from fat), Total Fat 6 g, Saturated Fat 3 g, Protein 1 g, Carbohydrate 5 g, Cholesterol 10 mg, Fiber 0 g, Sodium 45 mg, Sugars 0 g

Almond Cheesecake Bars

After-School Butterscotch Brownies

Almond Cheesecake Bars

Crust:

- ¼ cup SPLENDA® No Calorie Sweetener, Granulated
- 1¼ cups graham cracker or vanilla wafer crumbs
- ⅓ cup light butter, melted
- ¼ cup toasted sliced almonds, finely ground

Filling:

- 12 ounces reduced-fat cream cheese
- ½ cup SPLENDA® No Calorie Sweetener, Granulated
- 2 large eggs
- ¼ cup reduced-fat sour cream

- 2½ teaspoons vanilla extract
- 1 teaspoon almond extract
- ¼ cup toasted, sliced almonds

1. Preheat oven to 350°F. Spray an 8-inch square baking pan with nonstick cooking spray. Set aside.

2. Prepare Crust. Mix crust ingredients together in a mixing bowl. Mix well. Press into prepared pan. Bake 10 to 12 minutes or until firm.

3. Prepare Filling. Mix cream cheese and SPLENDA® Granulated Sweetener together until smooth. Add eggs, one at a time, scraping the sides of the bowl and mixing well after each addition. Add sour cream and extracts; mix well. Pour over prepared crust.

4. Bake in preheated oven 40 to 47 minutes or until firm.

5. Top with toasted almonds.

Makes 20 servings
1 (1.6-inch × 2-inch) bar

PREP TIME: 15 minutes
COOK TIME: 59 minutes
TOTAL TIME: 1 hour, 14 minutes

Nutrition Information per Serving:
Calories 110 (70 calories from fat), Total Fat 8 g, Saturated Fat 4 g, Protein 4 g, Carbohydrate 7 g, Cholesterol 35 mg, Fiber 0 g, Sodium 105 mg, Sugars 3 g

After-School Butterscotch Brownies

- 2¼ cups all-purpose flour
- 1 teaspoon baking powder
- ½ teaspoon salt
- 1 cup butter or margarine, softened
- ¾ cup SPLENDA® Brown Sugar Blend, packed
- 1 tablespoon vanilla extract
- 2 large eggs
- 1 (11-ounce package) NESTLÉ® TOLL HOUSE® Butterscotch Flavored Morsels, divided
- ½ cup chopped pecans

1. Preheat oven to 350°F.

2. Combine flour, baking powder and salt in medium bowl. Set aside.

3. Combine butter, SPLENDA® Brown Sugar Blend and vanilla in a large mixing bowl; beat at medium speed until creamy. Beat in eggs. Gradually beat in flour mixture. Stir in 1 cup morsels and pecans. Spread into an ungreased 13×9-inch baking pan. Sprinkle with remaining ⅔ cup morsels.

4. Bake in preheated oven 30 to 40 minutes or until wooden pick inserted in center comes out clean. Cool in pan on wire rack. Cut into bars.

Makes 48 servings
1 (1.5-inch-square) bar

PREP TIME: 10 minutes
COOK TIME: 30 minutes
TOTAL TIME: 40 minutes

Nutrition Information per Serving:
Calories 120 (60 calories from fat), Total Fat 7 g, Saturated Fat 4 g, Protein 1 g, Carbohydrate 12 g, Cholesterol 20 mg, Fiber 0 g, Sodium 75 mg, Sugars 7 g

Oat-Date Bars

Coconut-Date-Nut Balls

Oat-Date Bars

- 8 ounces chopped dates
- ¾ cup NESTLÉ® CARNATION® Lowfat 2% Evaporated Milk
- 1 tablespoon SPLENDA® Sugar Blend
- 1 teaspoon vanilla extract
- 1 cup all-purpose flour
- ¾ cup quick-cooking oats
- ½ teaspoon baking soda
- ½ teaspoon salt
- ½ teaspoon ground cinnamon
- ½ cup butter or margarine, softened
- ¼ cup SPLENDA® Brown Sugar Blend, packed

1. Preheat oven to 400°F. Spray an 8-inch square baking pan with nonstick cooking spray.

2. Combine dates, evaporated milk, SPLENDA® Sugar Blend and vanilla in medium saucepan. Cook on medium-low heat, stirring occasionally, 8 to 10 minutes or until thickened. Remove from heat.

3. Combine flour, oats, baking soda, salt and cinnamon in a medium bowl. Set aside.

4. Combine butter and SPLENDA® Brown Sugar Blend in large bowl; beat at medium speed until creamy. Beat in flour mixture. With floured fingers, press half of crust mixture onto bottom of prepared baking pan. Spread date filling over crust. Top with remaining crust mixture.

5. Bake in preheated oven 20 to 25 minutes or until golden. Cut into bars. Serve warm.

Makes 16 servings
1 (2-inch-square) bar

PREP TIME: 15 minutes
COOK TIME: 20 minutes
TOTAL TIME: 35 minutes

Nutrition Information per Serving:
Calories 160 (60 calories from fat), Total Fat 6 g, Saturated Fat 4 g, Protein 3 g, Carbohydrate 24 g, Cholesterol 20 mg, Fiber 2 g, Sodium 190 mg, Sugars 14 g

Coconut-Date-Nut Balls

- ¾ cup flaked coconut
- ½ cup butter
- 1 (8-ounce) package dates, chopped
- ¾ cup chopped pecans
- ½ cup egg substitute
- ¾ cup SPLENDA® No Calorie Sweetener, Granulated
- 3½ cups crispy rice cereal

1. Preheat oven to 350°F. Bake coconut, stirring occasionally, 5 to 6 minutes or until toasted. Set aside.

2. Melt butter in a large skillet over low heat. Add dates and pecans; cook over low heat, stirring constantly until dates are softened. Cool to touch (about 5 minutes).

3. Beat egg substitute and SPLENDA® Granulated Sweetener for 3 minutes at medium speed with an electric mixer; add to date mixture. Cook over low heat, stirring constantly, until mixture thickens (about 3 minutes). Stir in rice cereal. Cool to touch.

Shape into 1-inch balls. Roll in toasted coconut.

Makes 36 servings
1 ball

PREP TIME: 10 minutes
COOK TIME: 14 minutes
TOTAL TIME: 24 minutes

Nutrition Information per Serving:
Calories 80 (45 calories from fat), Total Fat 5 g, Saturated Fat 2 g, Protein 1 g, Carbohydrate 8 g, Cholesterol 5 mg, Fiber 1 g, Sodium 55 mg, Sugars 5 g

Peanut Butter and Jelly Bites

Peanut Butter Cookie Bites

Peanut Butter and Jelly Bites

Peanut Butter Balls:

- 1 **stick SPLENDA® No Calorie Sweetener Flavors for Coffee, Caramel**
- 1 **stick SPLENDA® No Calorie Sweetener Flavors for Coffee, French Vanilla**
- 1 **tablespoon sugar-free cocoa mix**
- 1 **tablespoon graham cracker crumbs**
- 2 **tablespoons peanut butter**
- 1½ **teaspoons fat-free cream cheese**

Garnish:

- 2 **tablespoons graham cracker crumbs**
- 2 **teaspoons sugar-free or no-sugar-added jam**

1. Mix all peanut butter ball ingredients together in a small bowl. Roll into 6 balls. Roll balls in graham cracker crumbs.

2. Press a small indentation in center with fingertip. Fill with jam. Serve immediately.

Makes 2 servings
3 prepared bites

PREP TIME: 10 minutes
TOTAL TIME: 10 minutes

Nutrition Information per Serving:
Calories 150 (80 calories from fat), Total Fat 9 g, Saturated Fat 2 g, Protein 6 g, Carbohydrate 15 g, Cholesterol 0 mg, Fiber 1 g, Sodium 170 mg, Sugars 5 g

Peanut Butter Cookie Bites

- ¼ **cup margarine, softened**
- 1 **cup creamy peanut butter**
- ¼ **cup egg substitute**
- 2 **tablespoons honey**
- ½ **teaspoon vanilla extract**
- 1 **cup SPLENDA® No Calorie Sweetener, Granulated**
- 1½ **cups all-purpose flour**
- ½ **teaspoon baking soda**
- ½ **teaspoon salt**

1. Preheat oven to 350°F.

2. Beat margarine and peanut butter in a large mixing bowl with an electric mixer until creamy, approximately 1 minute.

3. Add egg substitute, honey and vanilla. Beat on high speed for approximately 1½ minutes.

4. Add SPLENDA® Granulated Sweetener and beat on medium speed until well blended, approximately 30 seconds.

5. Combine flour, baking soda and salt in a small mixing bowl. Slowly add flour mixture to peanut butter mixture, beating on low speed until well blended, about 1½ minutes. Mixture may be crumbly.

6. Roll level tablespoons of dough into balls and drop onto a lightly oiled or parchment-lined cookie sheet, 2 inches apart. Flatten each ball with a fork, pressing a crisscross pattern into each cookie. Bake in preheated oven 7 to 9 minutes or until light brown around the edges. Cool on wire rack.

Makes 24 servings
1 prepared bite

PREP TIME: 20 minutes
COOK TIME: 9 minutes
TOTAL TIME: 29 minutes

Nutrition Information per Serving:
Calories 120 (70 calories from fat), Total Fat 8 g, Saturated Fat 1 g, Protein 4 g, Carbohydrate 10 g, Cholesterol 0 mg, Fiber 1 g, Sodium 150 mg, Sugars 2 g

S'mores Campfire Pie

Apple Cranberry Pie

S'mores Campfire Pie

Filling:

- ½ **cup SPLENDA® Sugar Blend**
- ⅓ **cup fat-free half and half**
- 1 **teaspoon vanilla extract**
- 4 **(1-ounce) squares unsweetened chocolate, chopped**
- 1 **(9-inch) graham cracker crust**

Meringue:

- 4 **egg whites**
- ¼ **teaspoon cream of tartar**
- 1 **teaspoon vanilla extract**
- ½ **cup SPLENDA® Sugar Blend**

1. Prepare Filling. Combine SPLENDA® Sugar Blend and half and half in a small saucepan. Cook over medium heat, stirring constantly, until SPLENDA® Sugar Blend dissolves. Stir in vanilla; add chocolate, stirring until chocolate melts. Pour mixture into crust. Set aside.

2. Preheat oven to 225°F.

3. Prepare Meringue. Combine egg whites, cream of tartar and vanilla in a large mixing bowl; beat at high speed with an electric mixer until foamy. Gradually add SPLENDA® Sugar Blend, 1 tablespoon at a time, beating until stiff peaks form and SPLENDA® Sugar Blend dissolves. Spread meringue evenly over chocolate filling.

4. Bake in preheated oven 2 hours. Turn oven off and leave in oven, with door closed and oven light on, for 8 hours or overnight.

Makes 8 servings
1 slice (⅛ pie)

PREP TIME: 15 minutes
COOK TIME: 2 hours
TOTAL TIME: 10 hours, 15 minutes

Nutrition Information per Serving:
Calories 340 (130 calories from fat), Total Fat 14 g, Saturated Fat 6 g, Protein 5 g, Carbohydrate 46 g, Cholesterol 0 mg, Fiber 3 g, Sodium 190 mg, Sugars 37 g

Apple Cranberry Pie

- 1 **(15-ounce) package refrigerated pie crusts**
- ½ **cup SPLENDA® No Calorie Sweetener, Granulated**
- 1 **tablespoon all-purpose flour**
- ½ **teaspoon ground cinnamon**
- 4 **large Granny Smith apples, peeled, cored and sliced**
- 1 **cup cranberries, coarsely chopped**

1. Preheat oven to 400°F.

2. Unfold 1 pie crust; press out fold lines. Fit pie crust into a 9-inch pie plate according to package directions.

3. Combine SPLENDA® Granulated Sweetener, flour and cinnamon in a large bowl; add apples and cranberries, tossing gently. Spoon mixture into pie crust.

4. Unfold remaining pie crust; press out fold lines. Roll to ⅛-inch thickness. Place over filling; fold edges under and crimp. Cut slits in top to allow steam to escape.

5. Bake 40 to 50 minutes or until crust is golden. Cover edges with aluminum foil to prevent overbrowning, if necessary. Cool on a wire rack 1 hour before serving.

Makes 8 servings
1 slice (⅛ pie)

PREP TIME: 30 minutes
COOK TIME: 50 minutes
TOTAL TIME: 1 hour, 20 minutes

Nutrition Information per Serving:
Calories 290 (130 calories from fat), Total Fat 14 g, Saturated Fat 6 g, Protein 2 g, Carbohydrate 41 g, Cholesterol 10 mg, Fiber 3 g, Sodium 200 mg, Sugars 13 g

Nostalgic Apple Pie

Berry-Cherry Pie

Nostalgic Apple Pie

- 1 **(15-ounce) package refrigerated pie crusts**
- 7 **cups baking apples, peeled, cored and thinly sliced**
- 1 **cup SPLENDA® No Calorie Sweetener, Granulated**
- 3 **tablespoons cornstarch**
- ¾ **teaspoon ground cinnamon**
- ¼ **teaspoon ground nutmeg**
- ⅛ **teaspoon salt**

1. Preheat oven to 425°F.

2. Unfold 1 pie crust; press out fold lines. Fit pie crust into a 9-inch pie plate according to package directions.

3. Place sliced apples into a large mixing bowl; set aside. Combine SPLENDA® Granulated Sweetener, cornstarch, cinnamon, nutmeg and salt in a small bowl. Sprinkle mixture over apples and toss. Spoon apple mixture into pie crust. Place the second crust over the filling. Seal edges, trim and flute. Cut small slits in top to allow steam to escape.

4. Bake in preheated oven 40 to 50 minutes or until the crust is golden. Serve warm or chilled.

Makes 8 servings
1 slice (⅛ pie)

PREP TIME: 15 minutes
COOK TIME: 50 minutes
TOTAL TIME: 1 hour, 5 minutes

Nutrition Information per Serving:
Calories 300 (140 calories from fat), Total Fat 15 g, Saturated Fat 4 g, Protein 3 g, Carbohydrate 40 g, Cholesterol 0 mg, Fiber 5 g, Sodium 270 mg, Sugars 14 g

Berry-Cherry Pie

- 1 **(15-ounce) package refrigerated pie crusts**
- 1 **(14.5-ounce) can pitted tart red cherries, undrained**
- 1 **(12-ounce) package frozen raspberries, thawed**
- 1 **cup fresh blueberries or frozen blueberries, thawed**
- 1 **cup SPLENDA® No Calorie Sweetener, Granulated**
- ¼ **cup cornstarch**
- 2 **tablespoons butter**

  Optional topping: frozen low-fat vanilla yogurt

1. Preheat oven to 375°F.

2. Unfold 1 pie crust; press out fold lines. Fit pie crust into a 9-inch pie plate according to package directions.

3. Drain cherries, raspberries and blueberries (if frozen), reserving 1 cup of the juices. Set berries and juice aside.

4. Combine SPLENDA® Granulated Sweetener and cornstarch in a medium saucepan; gradually stir in reserved juice. Cook over medium heat, stirring constantly until mixture begins to boil. Boil 1 minute, stirring constantly. Stir in butter and reserved fruit. Cool slightly and spoon mixture into pie shell.

5. Unroll remaining pie crust; roll to ⅛-inch thickness. Place over filling. Seal edges, trim and flute. Cut slits in top to allow steam to escape.

6. Bake in preheated oven 40 to 45 minutes or until crust is golden. Cover edges with aluminum foil to prevent overbrowning, if necessary. Cool on a wire rack. Serve with a scoop of frozen yogurt, if desired.

Makes 8 servings
1 slice (⅛ pie)

PREP TIME: 25 minutes
COOK TIME: 45 minutes
TOTAL TIME: 1 hour, 10 minutes

Nutrition Information per Serving:
Calories 330 (170 calories from fat), Total Fat 19 g, Saturated Fat 6 g, Protein 4 g, Carbohydrate 37 g, Cholesterol 10 mg, Fiber 4 g, Sodium 290 mg, Sugars 7 g

Chocolate Velvet Mousse

Easy Pumpkin Pie

Chocolate Velvet Mousse

- 3 ounces unsweetened chocolate
- 1 cup 1% low-fat milk
- ¼ cup egg substitute
- ½ cup SPLENDA® No Calorie Sweetener, Granulated
- 1 teaspoon cornstarch
- 2 tablespoons orange-flavored liqueur or brandy*
- ½ cup heavy cream
- 3 cups sliced strawberries

For dietary purposes, please note that this recipe contains alcohol. Alcohol can be replaced with 1 teaspoon orange extract.

1. Place chocolate and milk in a medium saucepan. Heat over medium heat until chocolate melts. Set aside.

2. Stir together egg substitute, SPLENDA® Granulated Sweetener, cornstarch and orange-flavored liqueur or brandy in a small mixing bowl. Add to chocolate mixture. Stir constantly. Cook over medium heat while stirring constantly, until mixture begins to thicken (approximately 3 to 4 minutes). Remove from heat and pour into the bowl of a blender or food processor. Blend or process briefly (10 to 20 seconds) to make a more creamy texture. Pour into medium bowl and cover.

3. Refrigerate chocolate mixture approximately 2 to 3 hours or until cool. Whip cream until stiff and fold into chocolate. Refrigerate overnight to set. Mousse will keep, refrigerated, for 3 days.

4. To serve, layer strawberries and mousse in 6 all-purpose wine glasses.

Makes 6 servings
¾ cup mousse, ½ cup strawberries

PREP TIME: 25 minutes
TOTAL TIME: 8 hours, 25 minutes

Nutrition Information per Serving:
Calories 210 (150 calories from fat), Total Fat 17 g, Saturated Fat 10 g, Protein 5 g, Carbohydrate 14 g, Cholesterol 30 mg, Fiber 4 g, Sodium 50 mg, Sugars 5 g

Easy Pumpkin Pie

- ¾ cup SPLENDA® No Calorie Sweetener, Granulated
- 2 tablespoons light molasses
- ¼ teaspoon salt
- 2 teaspoons ground cinnamon
- 4 egg whites
- 1 (15-ounce) can pumpkin purée
- 1¼ cups nonfat evaporated milk
- 1 (9-inch) unbaked pie crust
- 2 cups fat-free frozen whipped topping, thawed

1. Preheat oven to 350°F.

2. In a large mixing bowl, stir together SPLENDA® Granulated Sweetener, molasses, salt and cinnamon. Mix well. Stir in egg whites, pumpkin and milk. Pour into pie crust.

3. Bake in preheated oven 1¼ to 1½ hours or until a toothpick inserted into the pie comes out clean. Top with whipped topping before serving.

Makes 8 servings
1 slice (⅛ pie)

PREP TIME: 10 minutes
COOK TIME: 1 hour, 15 minutes
TOTAL TIME: 1 hour, 25 minutes

Nutrition Information per Serving:
Calories 220 (70 calories from fat), Total Fat 8 g, Saturated Fat 2 g, Protein 7 g, Carbohydrate 29 g, Cholesterol 0 mg, Fiber 3 g, Sodium 400 mg, Sugars 16 g

Frozen Mini Cinnamon
Coffee Cheesecakes

Fresh Strawberry Pie

Frozen Mini Cinnamon Coffee Cheesecakes

- 12 NABISCO® Ginger Snaps
- 2 tablespoons MAXWELL HOUSE® Naturally Decaffeinated Instant Coffee
- 1 tablespoon water
- ½ cup SPLENDA® No Calorie Sweetener, Granulated
- 1 (8-ounce) container PHILADELPHIA® Light Cream Cheese Spread
- 1 teaspoon vanilla extract
- ¼ teaspoon ground cinnamon
- 1½ cups thawed COOL WHIP® Whipped Topping
- 1 cup fresh raspberries

1. Line 12 muffin tin cups with paper liners. Place 1 cookie in each paper cup. Set aside.

2. Mix coffee granules and water in large bowl until coffee is dissolved. Add SPLENDA® Granulated Sweetener, cream cheese spread, vanilla and cinnamon. Beat with wire whisk until well blended. Gently stir in whipped topping.

3. Spoon mixture evenly over cookies in muffin pan. Top each cheesecake with raspberries. Cover and freeze for 3 hours or overnight.

4. Remove from freezer about 10 minutes before serving to soften slightly.

Makes 12 servings
1 mini cheesecake

PREP TIME: 15 minutes
TOTAL TIME: 3 hours, 15 minutes

Nutrition Information per Serving:
Calories 35 (18 calories from fat), Total Fat 2 g, Saturated Fat 2 g, Protein 0 g, Carbohydrate 3 g, Cholesterol 0 mg, Fiber 1 g, Sodium 0 mg, Sugars 2 g

Fresh Strawberry Pie

- ⅓ cup water
- 1 cup SPLENDA® No Calorie Sweetener, Granulated
- 1 (1-ounce) package unflavored gelatin
- ⅓ cup water
- 6 cups strawberries, cleaned and cut in half
- 1 (9-inch) prepared reduced-fat graham cracker crust

1. Pour ⅓ cup water in a small mixing bowl. Add SPLENDA® Granulated Sweetener. Stir well. Sprinkle gelatin over the top. Let stand 1 minute.

2. Pour ⅓ cup water in a small pan. Boil. Pour boiling water over gelatin mixture. Stir until dissolved.

3. Refrigerate approximately 20 minutes or until the mixture begins to thicken. Stir frequently.

4. Toss with prepared berries and spoon into pie crust. Chill until set.

Makes 8 servings
1 slice (⅛ pie)

PREP TIME: 20 minutes
TOTAL TIME: 50 minutes

Nutrition Information per Serving:
Calories 140 (35 calories from fat), Total Fat 4 g, Saturated Fat 1 g, Protein 5 g, Carbohydrate 22 g, Cholesterol 0 mg, Fiber 3 g, Sodium 95 mg, Sugars 6 g

Banana Punch Slush

Caramel Latte

Banana Punch Slush

4 ripe bananas
¾ cup SPLENDA® No Calorie Sweetener, Granulated
6 cups water, divided
1 (46-fluid-ounce) can pineapple juice
2 (12-fluid-ounce) cans frozen orange juice concentrate
1 (12-fluid-ounce) can frozen lemonade concentrate
3 liters ginger ale

1. In a blender, combine bananas, SPLENDA® Granulated Sweetener and 3 cups water. Blend until smooth. Pour into a large bowl and stir in pineapple juice. Stir in orange juice concentrate, lemonade concentrate and 3 more cups water. Divide into 3 plastic containers and freeze until solid.

2. Remove from freezer 3 to 4 hours before serving. Using 1 portion at a time, place slush in a punch bowl and pour in 1 liter of ginger ale for each.

Makes 54 servings
1 (4-fluid-ounce) drink

PREP TIME: 15 minutes
TOTAL TIME: 3 hours, 15 minutes

Nutrition Information per Serving:
Calories 80 (0 calories from fat),
Total Fat 0 g, Saturated Fat 0 g,
Protein 0 g, Carbohydrate 19 g,
Cholesterol 0 mg, Fiber 0 g,
Sodium 10 mg, Sugars 18 g

Caramel Latte

2 sticks SPLENDA® Flavors for Coffee, Caramel
¼ cup brewed espresso
¼ teaspoon vanilla extract
½ cup 2% reduced-fat milk

1. Mix all ingredients together in a microwaveable bowl or mug. Heat in microwave 30 to 40 seconds or to desired temperature.

2. Blend in blender 15 to 20 seconds to create a frothy drink, if desired. Pour into serving cup and serve immediately.

Makes 1 serving
1 (6-fluid-ounce) drink

PREP TIME: 5 minutes
TOTAL TIME: 5 minutes

Nutrition Information per Serving:
Calories 70 (20 calories from fat),
Total Fat 2 g, Saturated Fat 2 g,
Protein 4 g, Carbohydrate 9 g,
Cholesterol 10 mg, Fiber 0 g,
Sodium 70 mg, Sugars 6 g

Banana Strawberry Shake

KOOL-AID® Fizzy Float

Banana Strawberry Shake

- 1 large ripe banana, sliced
- 5 packets SPLENDA® No Calorie Sweetener
- ½ cup 2% reduced-fat milk
- 1¼ cups frozen unsweetened strawberries

1. Combine all ingredients in a blender. Blend on medium speed until smooth.

2. Pour into glasses and serve.

Makes 2 servings
1 (8-fluid-ounce) drink

PREP TIME: 5 minutes
TOTAL TIME: 5 minutes

Nutrition Information per Serving:
Calories 140 (15 calories from fat), Total Fat 2 g, Saturated Fat 1 g, Protein 3 g, Carbohydrate 31 g, Cholesterol 5 mg, Fiber 5 g, Sodium 35 mg, Sugars 25 g

KOOL-AID® Fizzy Float

- 1 quart cold water
- 2 cups light white grape juice, chilled
- 1 cup SPLENDA® No Calorie Sweetener, Granulated
- 1 envelope of your favorite flavor KOOL-AID® Unsweetened Soft Drink Mix
- 2 cups seltzer water, chilled
- 2 cups no-sugar-added light vanilla ice cream

1. Combine water, grape juice, SPLENDA® Granulated Sweetener and KOOL-AID® Soft Drink Mix in a pitcher, stirring until SPLENDA® Granulated Sweetener dissolves.

2. Pour ¾ cup of the mixture into each of 8 tall glasses; add ¼ cup of the seltzer to each glass. Top each serving with ¼ cup of the ice cream. Serve immediately. Store leftover prepared drink in refrigerator.

Makes 8 servings
1 (8-fluid-ounce) drink

PREP TIME: 10 minutes
TOTAL TIME: 10 minutes

Nutrition Information per Serving:
Calories 70 (20 calories from fat), Total Fat 2 g, Saturated Fat 1 g, Protein 1 g, Carbohydrate 15 g, Cholesterol 5 mg, Fiber 0 g, Sodium 40 mg, Sugars 7 g

Caramel Apple Cider

Virgin Mojito

Caramel Apple Cider

- 1 stick SPLENDA® No Calorie Sweetener Flavors for Coffee, Caramel
- 2 sticks SPLENDA® No Calorie Sweetener Flavors for Coffee, Cinnamon Spice
- 1 cup apple cider or apple juice

Mix all ingredients together in a large mug or coffee cup. Heat in microwave until warm. Serve immediately.

Makes 1 serving
1 (8-fluid-ounce) drink

PREP TIME: 5 minutes
TOTAL TIME: 5 minutes

Nutrition Information per Serving:
Calories 120 (0 calories from fat), Total Fat 0 g, Saturated Fat 0 g, Protein 0 g, Carbohydrate 32 g, Cholesterol 0 mg, Fiber 0 g, Sodium 25 mg, Sugars 26 g

Virgin Mojito

- 6 mint leaves
- 1 tablespoon SPLENDA® No Calorie Sweetener, Granulated
- 1 lime, juiced
- 1 (12-ounce) can diet lemon-lime soda, chilled
- Fresh mint for garnish (optional)
- Lime slices for garnish (optional)

1. Smash mint leaves and SPLENDA® Granulated Sweetener with a spoon in the bottom of a large glass.

2. Add lime juice and stir. Pour in soda and stir well.* Garnish with mint and lime slices, if desired. Serve chilled.

*A cocktail shaker can be used to create a frothier beverage. Add ice and mojito to a shaker and shake well.

Makes 1 serving
1 (12-fluid-ounce) drink

PREP TIME: 5 minutes
TOTAL TIME: 5 minutes

Nutrition Information per Serving:
Calories 20 (0 calories from fat), Total Fat 0 g, Saturated Fat 0 g, Protein 0 g, Carbohydrate 6 g, Cholesterol 0 mg, Fiber 0 g, Sodium 55 mg, Sugars 3 g

Mock Sangria

Berry Simple Smoothie

Mock Sangria

- 2 sticks SPLENDA® No Calorie Sweetener FLAVOR ACCENTS™, Lemon
- 1 thin slice fresh lemon
- 2 thin slices fresh orange
- 1 cup alcohol-removed wine
- 3 thin slices fresh apple
  Ice, as desired

Crush SPLENDA® No Calorie Sweetener FLAVOR ACCENTS™, lemon and orange slices with a fork in a tall glass. Add wine and stir. Add apple slices and ice, as desired. Serve immediately.

Makes 1 serving
1 (8-fluid-ounce) drink

PREP TIME: 5 minutes
TOTAL TIME: 5 minutes

Nutrition Information per Serving:
Calories 35 (0 calories from fat), Total Fat 0 g, Saturated Fat 0 g, Protein 1 g, Carbohydrate 10 g, Cholesterol 0 mg, Fiber 1 g, Sodium 25 mg, Sugars 7 g

Berry Simple Smoothie

- 2 cups frozen unsweetened whole strawberries
- 1 cup fat-free plain yogurt
- ½ cup lite cranberry juice
- ¼ cup SPLENDA® No Calorie Sweetener, Granulated

Combine frozen strawberries, yogurt, cranberry juice and SPLENDA® Granulated Sweetener in a blender until smooth, stopping to scrape down sides.

Makes 3 servings
about 1 cup

PREP TIME: 5 minutes
TOTAL TIME: 5 minutes

Nutrition Information per Serving:
Calories 110 (0 calories from fat), Total Fat 0 g, Saturated Fat 0 g, Protein 5 g, Carbohydrate 22 g, Cholesterol 0 mg, Fiber 3 g, Sodium 65 mg, Sugars 18 g

Strawberry Orange Smash Smoothie

Raspberry Hot Chocolate

Strawberry Orange Smash Smoothie

3 cups frozen strawberries, unsweetened

⅔ cup SPLENDA® No Calorie Sweetener, Granulated

1¼ cups orange juice, calcium fortified

1 cup plain nonfat yogurt

½ teaspoon vanilla extract

¼ cup ice cubes

Add all ingredients to blender. Blender will be full. Mix on low speed for 10 seconds. Remove lid, stir with wooden spoon. Mix on medium speed 15 to 20 seconds; remove lid and stir again. Mix on high speed 15 to 20 seconds or until smooth. Pour into glasses. Serve immediately.

Makes 5 servings
1 (8-fluid-ounce) drink

PREP TIME: 10 minutes
TOTAL TIME: 10 minutes

Nutrition Information per Serving:
Calories 80 (0 calories from fat), Total Fat 0 g, Saturated Fat 0 g, Protein 3 g, Carbohydrate 19 g, Cholesterol 0 mg, Fiber 2 g, Sodium 30 mg, Sugars 14 g

Raspberry Hot Chocolate

2 sticks SPLENDA® No Calorie Sweetener FLAVOR ACCENTS™, Raspberry

1 packet sugar-free hot cocoa mix

1 cup 1% low-fat milk

1. Mix SPLENDA® No Calorie Sweetener FLAVOR ACCENTS™ and dry cocoa mix in a mug or coffee cup. Heat milk on stovetop or in microwave.

2. Pour hot milk into mug. Stir well. Serve immediately.

Makes 1 serving
1 (8-fluid-ounce) drink

PREP TIME: 2 minutes
TOTAL TIME: 2 minutes

Nutrition Information per Serving:
Calories 150 (25 calories from fat), Total Fat 3 g, Saturated Fat 2 g, Protein 12 g, Carbohydrate 22 g, Cholesterol 10 mg, Fiber 0 g, Sodium 220 mg, Sugars 19 g